T0285525

Praise for *Run Like Hell*

"As a licensed psychotherapist, EMDR-certified clinician, relational trauma therapy center founder, and relational trauma recovery expert, I highly endorse my colleague Nadine Macaluso, LMFT, PhD's, groundbreaking book, *Run Like Hell*. This book sheds light on the dark issue of intimate partner violence and trauma bonding, revealing the insidious threads that weave victims into the fabric of abuse. Dr. Macaluso adeptly navigates the complex landscape of intimate partner violence, emphasizing the urgent need to recognize it as profound relational trauma, an under-discussed but extremely important topic. This book sets itself apart not only by its unwavering commitment to bringing this issue to the forefront and addressing the misconceptions surrounding it but also by the vulnerable and generous modeling of the author—a woman who lived through this herself and whose life and story have been made famous in recent years. It's through data, statistics, and her generous personal shares that Dr. Macaluso shows us that intimate partner violence affects people of all ages, genders, and socio-economic backgrounds, reminding us of the pervasive nature of intimate partner violence and the profoundly detrimental impact it can have if left unaddressed. As a relational trauma therapist, I have seen firsthand the courage of IPV survivors striving to break free from the chains of trauma bonding. This book validates their experiences and provides an empathetic road map for understanding the complex dynamics at play. Each chapter equips readers with a profound awareness of this issue, making it an essential read for all. But also, as someone who has lived through relational trauma and who witnessed intimate partner violence in my family of origin, I'll say that, personally, this is the book I wish my own mother had access to 35 years ago . . . I am so grateful that Dr. Macaluso has written this book, and I have no doubt that it will positively impact the lives of many individuals and their children for years to come."

—ANNIE WRIGHT, LMFT, www.anniewright.com

"Dr. Nae's book provides invaluable information and insights into toxic relationships and trauma bonds. She beautifully explains how we can end up in trauma bonds, signs to recognize, and ways to safely get out of and break free from trauma bonds while normalizing how unfortunately common it is to experience a trauma bond relationship. Through her helpful takeaways at the end of every chapter, stories of toxic relationships, and her personal experience, Dr. Nae's compassion for any woman in a TBR is felt throughout the book. She eloquently breaks through any shame and offers empathy, understanding, insight, and practical tools to identify and escape trauma bond relationships. She highlights the importance of the mind-body connection and ways we can take care of ourselves to heal and overcome the impact of trauma bonds. This book is essential for anyone who feels they may be in a toxic relationship or working on breaking free from trauma bond relationships. It is also incredibly valuable for young adults entering relationships to gain awareness of toxic relationship patterns to ensure that they can recognize toxic traits and set healthy boundaries. As a therapist who specializes in working with children and families who have experienced trauma bonds and toxic relationships, I appreciate Dr. Nae writing this book to bring more awareness to the impact these relationships have on the family and the importance of finding a therapist who is well trained and experienced in trauma-informed care."

—DR. JULIE PAYNE, DMFT, LMFT,
licensed marriage and family therapist

"*Run Like Hell* is a book for anyone who loves. If you are beginning to date, questioning things you encounter in a current relationship, or going back to dating after divorce—this book is for you. From Nadine's recounting of key details from her own treacherous climb out of a toxic relationship, I was given a healthy dose of understanding, support, education, community (actual accounts of many women's struggles), and much-needed empowerment. She goes on to provide evidence-based information and functional tools to use to ensure we all get what we deserve: Love. This book is the perfect blend of comfort and the mental exercises you need to give you the stamina to run like hell from a toxic relationship."

—KELLYLYN LANDRUS,
teacher and trauma bond surthriver

"Nadine's book was no less than pivotal in helping me leave an abusive, trauma bond relationship. I realized I wasn't alone, I wasn't crazy, and there was a way to heal! It gave me the tools I needed and the courage and strength to keep going. Nadine's book should be on everyone's bookshelf! Know the signs. Heed the red flags. And if you are in a trauma bond, it will give you the hope, strength, courage, and tools not only to leave but to rebuild your life. I am going to send every girlfriend of mine a copy! It's a must-have!"

—VICKY EDWARDS, trauma bond surthriver

A Therapist's Guide *to* Recognizing,
Escaping, *and* Healing *from* Trauma Bonds

RUN
LIKE
HELL

NADINE MACALUSO, LMFT, PhD

GREENLEAF
BOOK GROUP PRESS

Published by Greenleaf Book Group Press
Austin, Texas
www.gbgpress.com

Copyright © 2024 Nadine Macaluso

All rights reserved.

Thank you for purchasing an authorized edition of this book
and for complying with copyright law. No part of this book may
be reproduced, stored in a retrieval system, or transmitted by
any means, electronic, mechanical, photocopying, recording, or
otherwise, without written permission from the copyright holder.

Distributed by Greenleaf Book Group

For ordering information or special discounts for bulk purchases,
please contact Greenleaf Book Group at PO Box 91869, Austin,
TX 78709, 512.891.6100.

Design and composition by Greenleaf Book Group
Cover design by Greenleaf Book Group and Matthew McRae
Cover images used under license from ©Shutterstock.com/
vectorisland

Publisher's Cataloging-in-Publication data is available.

Print ISBN: 979-8-88645-159-7

eBook ISBN: 979-8-88645-160-3

To offset the number of trees consumed in the printing of our books,
Greenleaf donates a portion of the proceeds from each printing to
the Arbor Day Foundation. Greenleaf Book Group has replaced over
50,000 trees since 2007.

Printed in the United States of America on acid-free paper

23 24 25 26 27 28 29 30   10 9 8 7 6 5 4 3 2 1

First Edition

Dedicated to my mother, Suzanne Marie Hogan

CONTENTS

Author's Note and Content Advisory

MY ROAD TO UNDERSTANDING TRAUMA bonds began after experiencing and escaping an abusive relationship with my first husband, the infamous Wolf of Wall Street. My passion for helping women in similar situations led me to not only become a psychotherapist but to write this book.

Please take into consideration that this book contains stories of abusive relationships with pathological partners, and it explores themes around trauma. My intention is never to glorify these abusive relationships, but to show readers they are not alone in their traumatic experiences and to provide illustrations of how to survive in and thrive after these relationships.

Foreword

by Christine Hammond, LMHC, NCC, leading mental health influencer, guest speaker, host of the popular podcast *Understanding Today's Narcissist*, and author of the award-winning *The Exhausted Woman's Handbook*

AS WOMEN, MOST OF US grew up knowing the Cinderella story. And as young girls, we often believed in the fairy tale: The idea that a handsome, charming prince would sweep you off your feet, pursue you with an endless passion, and rescue you from your worries, troubles, and sorrows. Surely, this instant, electric attraction would transform into a happily-ever-after relationship—a living example of fairy tales coming true. But there is a reason the Cinderella story ends with the wedding scene. Because so often, what started as a fairy tale ends in a nightmare.

If your Cinderella story has become a nightmare, empathy is not enough. You need someone who has experienced what you have. Not someone who is looking to see what is wrong with you and why you stayed in the toxic relationship. Because the truth is, for some toxic relationships, there is no warning and no red flags. There are no friends or family saying this person is dangerous.

That is why Dr. Nadine Macaluso has written this book: To gently guide you into realization, understanding, and healing from what probably seemed to be a fairy-tale relationship, through the nightmare abuse cycles, to the traumatic ending. In sharing her very public personal journey and the journeys of other trauma bond *surthrivers*, Nadine compassionately demonstrates that helping women heal from trauma bond relationships is more than a profession for her, it is her story as well.

Therapists like Dr. Nadine Macaluso are trained to show empathy for clients, but Nadine has been through the entire experience firsthand. She personally knows that even after the first abuse cycle begins, there is meaningful restitution, a belief that things will be better, and a hope that the relationship is simply going through growing pains. But then it happens again, followed by another period of intimacy and connection. Friends and family don't see what is happening, which intensifies a woman's feelings of doubt, shame, and isolation. As the cycles increase in intensity and frequency, gaslighting, blaming, and guilt-tripping become the norm. With the passing of time, comes a change in who you are as a woman, what you believe, and how you respond.

This is exactly where a pathological lover wants you. Bendable to their wants and desires, accommodating to their needs, and giving all of yourself to someone who gives little in return. It is hard to see from the inside of the relationship where you are and how you have gotten here. And even harder to get out.

Impossible, really, without assistance or guidance.

This book is your guidance. It is the light at the end of your nightmare, waking you up from the bad dream that has become your reality. If this book is not your story, it might be a friend's story. Giving them this book might just save their life. Whether this book speaks to you or someone you know, it will show you the path toward healing and a return to your true nature.

Preface

IT WAS MY PERSONAL HEARTBREAK that led to my professional interest in traumatic bonding between lovers. After living through my own traumatic bond with a pathological lover, I became obsessed with finding answers: Why did my ex act the way he did? How could someone like me—a smart and empathetic woman—have fallen for him? How and why had I stayed with him? And how could I avoid getting into relationships with other people like him in the future? I also desperately wanted to help other women in the same types of relationships.

That's why, in the summer of 2010, I found myself composing these pages before I ever realized a book would emerge. I was writing my thesis to complete my master's degree in counseling to become a licensed marriage and family therapist. I used that research opportunity to write about my traumatic marriage to Jordan Belfort—the man portrayed onscreen in the movie *The Wolf of Wall Street* starring Leonardo DiCaprio. Although Leo's acting earned him an Academy Award nomination for Best Actor for playing the role of my former husband, I only saw the pain of my relationship playing out on the big screen for entertainment.

When it came time to write my thesis, topics included everything I'd experienced due to my marriage to Jordan—trauma, betrayal, loss of self, and personal growth. I then compared those archetypal themes to the Greek myth of Persephone. In 2010, terms such as trauma bonding and coercive control were barely used in academic psychological circles; I had no idea there were specific words for what I had endured with Jordan.

After completing that degree, I remained in school because I wanted to continue to learn about the mind, body, and soul. I earned my PhD in somatic psychotherapy—a science that bridges traditional psychotherapy with the body's wisdom—and wrote my dissertation on healing relational trauma or complex post-traumatic stress disorder (C-PTSD). C-PTSD is the formal diagnosis for a constellation of psychological and physical symptoms resulting from prolonged chronic exposure to traumatic adverse childhood experiences (ACEs) such as abuse or neglect.

I have spent most of my life studying lost, controlling, obsessive, and traumatic love. My fascination with love led me to become a therapist specializing in helping people recover from the pain of current or past relational trauma. Because I've been there. I know.

One of the first things I learned in school was that relational trauma occurs due to neglect or abuse between a parent and child or, in adulthood, between lovers. Regardless of the source of trauma, the very definition assumes that the person experiencing it did not have the resources to handle the situation. Therefore, relational trauma makes people feel powerless, helpless, and groundless.

In fact, the pain of heartbreak shows neurobiological evidence of stress, like torture. Having personally endured romantic trauma, I agree. This humbling experience of being married to the Wolf taught me the contrast between the sweetness of love and the tragedy of remaining innocent about its power. These two threads have interwoven in my life into an academic understanding of intimate love, self-love, traumatic bonding, and post-traumatic growth.

When I first met Jordan, I was a naive twenty-two-year-old. During our courtship, he showered me with compliments, over-the-top gifts, and seemingly utter devotion. I was swept up in this man's relentless, overwhelming pursuit, and against my better judgment, I caved to his constant pressure and agreed to marry him within six months of meeting and to immediately have children.

What followed was an eight-year toxic cycle of love, violence, and threats, an utterly confusing and harmful relationship that I later realized was a trauma bond relationship. After almost a decade of marriage to a violent, volatile drug addict, after countless scenes of trashed rooms, screamed threats in front of our two children, and living in fear, I finally found an opportunity to safely leave when the FBI placed Jordan under house arrest for money laundering. I knew then that he wouldn't be able to come after us. I left with my children and never looked back.

To this day, he has never made amends with me, and I have never demanded that he do so. I know now it isn't possible for him. As a result, we never genuinely connected again.

In the years that followed my divorce, psychotherapists labeled me as codependent and Jordan as an addict. Yet, I knew those categories were too simple and did not describe the depth of the agony I'd endured. As I've since learned, traumatic bonding is complex: the person who loves you repeatedly harms you and feels entitled to do so. It is confusing and terrifying.

As if surviving our Greek drama wasn't enough, Jordan further exploited my trauma by writing the book *The Wolf of Wall Street*, which then became a major motion picture. The world witnessed our trauma bonding through his narrative, but he didn't include my perspective. It was the ultimate form of gaslighting.

After the movie was released, I knew that one day I would write a book that finally told my side of the story—perhaps one that could help others, especially once I completed my education. And one day, my gut said, "Now is the time."

Another motivation was my therapy practice, which involves treating people in complex relationships. Looking back over the years, I have been astonished to realize that 75 percent of my female patients are in trauma-bonded relationships.

My therapy room reflects society. Millions of American women stay with lovers who violate them. Many of my patients complain that, in their prior therapy experiences, they have been labeled as codependent or enabling. Yet, I agree with abuse expert Lundy Bancroft, who wrote in *Why Does He Do That?*, "Abuse is a problem that lies entirely within the abuser."[1] I know because I was one of those women, so I deeply empathize with their pain, humiliation, and devastation.

Thus, I made it my mission to understand the whos, whats, hows, and whys. The successful navigation of my journey, combined with witnessing my patients' courage, now provides me with chances to be constantly in awe of how resilient we all are.

Seeing my likeness portrayed on the big screen alongside Leonardo DiCaprio was a public and humiliating mirror that most of my patients luckily do not have to endure. I have spent countless moments wondering, "Why me? Why did I go through a traumatic first marriage that nearly killed me?" And then I had to endure seeing that experience morph into a one-sided book and a movie that grossed over $500 million worldwide.

However, I've found the answer to the why. I presume we are all here for a purpose. As a wounded healer, I believe that we are all meant to be each other's supporters. I know that my suffering, growth, and education are intended to serve a larger goal: to educate women about the wolves wearing a mask of sanity that seduce them into a trauma bond, how to disengage if you are in a trauma bond, and, most notably, how to recover after one.

If you are reading this book, please know you are not alone. You belong to a large group of women engaging in this profound healing work. You also have light magic, which will help you face your trauma bond and see new possibilities. I hope this book invites you to enter the unknown territory of your healing process so that you can become a *surthriver.*

INTRODUCTION
The Paradox of Love

We are never so defenseless against suffering as when we love.[1]

—SIGMUND FREUD

ROMANTIC LOVE IS INTOXICATING AND crushing. We've all experienced this. Love involves amplified emotions and is complex, unique, and often irrational. We can idealize intimacy while fearing it. And if we are too thirsty for another's love, we can get lured into a trauma bond.

Traumatic bonding can occur between spouses, family members, bosses, and subordinates. This book, however, highlights traumatic bonding between lovers. Females tend to be more emotional than men, leaving them more susceptible to emotional dependence in relationships. Men can be victimized by their lovers too, yet in this book, I am focusing on women as victims based on research and professional experiences with my patients spanning more than a decade.

We are often pawns in a love game we do not understand. A trauma bond relationship (TBR) starts with promises of tenderness, trust, and safety between two seemingly honest individuals. Passion and obsession seal the bond. But what happens when your partner suddenly changes the game's rules? When his kindness and warmth become lies and threats? Your once-charming soulmate now feels like a possessive cellmate.

Do you recognize the following scenarios?

Confronting your partner drives him to accuse you. You begin defending yourself and questioning your sanity while toxic cycles of bliss followed by despair cause you to crave a deeper connection. Yet you are no match for his manipulation and domination. Left with no choice, you rationalize his abuse and minimize his betrayals because his unrelenting intimidation crushes your willpower.

As your well-being depends on the moments of peace you share with him, you begin to believe your well-being and safety depend on his love, so you compulsively accommodate his needs and deny yours. Feelings of dependency, tangled with forgiveness and denial, emotionally bond you to your intimate terrorist.

If you or someone you know has suffered through this—if you *are* suffering through this—you are not alone. You have been in a trauma bond.

Trauma bonds are *violent attachments*; they demonstrate the paradox of love.

MY WHY

Love is blind.

How many times have you heard that expression? Perhaps you said it to comfort a friend whose husband cheated on her. Maybe you've thought it after ending a seemingly idyllic relationship. Love can even make us blind to our blindness. We are not aware that we are missing anything. I said it to myself after reading an anonymous direct message on Instagram.

> Hi, I'm reaching out because I'm unsure what to do and need
> help. I am dating a narcissist, and I've been trying to leave

him. I've discovered that he's cheating on me, with a woman you know . . . a colleague of yours.

"A colleague of mine? Who in the world?" I kept reading.

I believe she has no idea he's involved with me. I have been internally fighting with telling her because he has threatened my job. I have seen through Instagram that she has introduced her children to him. He did the same with mine, which weighs on me since we both have been through high-conflict divorces. She's with a man whom she does not know at all. Thank you for reading.

I thought, "Well, Nae, it's official. You have become a Trauma Bond Whisperer." I don't recall aspiring to be a trauma bond whisperer. Nor did I earn my PhD to learn how a person emotionally bonds to an intimacy terrorist.

Yet, I reached out to the woman who sent me that DM, and she confirmed that my colleague's boyfriend had a whole secret life. Love's power compels us to see what we want rather than what is there.

Ugh! I felt sick telling my colleague that her boyfriend currently had another girlfriend and was possibly a pathological liar. Deception cloaked in devotion is hard to see. Even an expert can be seduced and conned (again) by a manipulative lover. Weekly, women desperately ask me why they fell into a trauma bond. How do they leave? Can they recover? And most importantly, how do they never, ever endure one again?

My therapy room is a relational lab that reflects society. After all, "domestic occurrences comprise the largest category of calls to the police in the United States."[2] I am sure you have seen R. Kelly, Harvey Weinstein, and Jeffrey Epstein splashed over the Internet. Intimate partner abuse in the United States continues unabated. It is a dangerous epidemic in this country that leaves a trail of wounded women and children.

This book is a universal answer for women everywhere.

WHAT CAN YOU EXPECT FROM THIS BOOK?

If you are trapped in a trauma bond or have survived one, this book will validate your experience by naming what you have endured. Unfortunately, some therapists are undertrained in recognizing trauma bonds and their effects on mental health. Post-abuse symptoms are extreme and confusing and can often result in a misdiagnosis.

For instance, if a woman is emotionally reactive and dramatic, she might appear to have a personality disorder. Or if she is hypervigilant because she is being stalked, she is paranoid. However, these are all normal reactions to living through traumatic bonding.

Trauma bond victims often feel crushing shame for enduring such abuse. Well-intentioned therapists often intensify their humiliation: "Why didn't you leave after the hundredth time he promised to change and didn't? Why do you act so helpless?" Such professionals don't understand how manipulative and abusive tactics break down willpower.

A trauma bond victim's accurate diagnosis is complex post-traumatic stress disorder (C-PTSD). C-PTSD is a distinct form of relational trauma involving chronic emotional or physical abuse over a prolonged period. Examples of C-PTSD include child abuse, intimate partner abuse, and human trafficking.[3]

Traumatic bonding is brainwashing developed through intimidation, coercion, isolation, and manipulation. Traumatic bonding is an emotional process. Initially, the perpetrator establishes trust and connection, then exploits trust by abusing or coercively controlling their lover.[4] After the abuse, the victim accommodates and pacifies her aggressor to salvage her well-being because she thinks the abuser is the only source of relief from her pain and fear. Ironically, this psychological process creates an emotional bond.

Unfortunately, time does not heal all wounds. Many women live their lives with captive hearts, alone in the emotional desert of psychic numbness. This doesn't have to be you. I understand how you feel, so this book offers solutions to help you and other women recover from a trauma bond.

Cycles of chronic relational trauma at the hands of someone you trust cause C-PTSD symptoms of shame, insecurity, anxiety, depression, cognitive dissonance, addiction, and lack of trust in oneself. I wrote my dissertation on treatment for C-PTSD. I completed my post-doctoral training in a modality designed to treat C-PTSD.

This book explains what you need to understand to avoid victimization from the painful aspects of traumatic bonding. It also offers information to gain a deeper understanding of your psychology so you can love wisely. And perhaps most importantly, it offers help on how to leave safely and recover from your trauma.

I have arranged the book to reflect my thinking about traumatic bonding. The book has three parts and ten chapters.

Part 1, "Dangerously in Love," describes the who, what, why, and how.

In Chapter 1, "What Your Mother Never Told You," I explain the two primary components of traumatic bonding: intermittent abuse and power imbalance. Four different women's experiences of traumatic bonding are narrated to show readers the diverse ways traumatic bonding can manifest.

Research has shown that we can tame what we can name. We are less likely to become traumatized when we see something or someone coming. Therefore, to help prevent future heartbreak, Chapter 2, "Is He Twisted or Tender?," describes the complex personality, mood disorders, and impulsive behaviors that enable the abuser to be an antisocial lover in a trauma bond relationship (TBR). TBR abusers are cunning and deceptive; they initially play at being warm, caring, and thought-ful partners. Yet this charming mask conceals their selfish nature and antagonistic personality.

Trauma bonds begin with a sweet seduction, have a middle phase of domination and manipulation, and dramatically end. I will give many examples of their toxic cycles of abuse, manipulation, and inevitable harm in Chapter 3, "Trauma Bonding."

Chapter 4, "Opposites Do Attract," clarifies the personality traits that put women at risk of becoming trapped in a TBR. I describe dis-tinct personality traits from the five-factor model of personality. These prosocial traits create stability and safety in healthy relationships yet get weaponized by a toxic partner.

Part 2, "Trauma Bond Free," explores the process of releasing the bonds of trauma. Chapter 5, "Emotional Scar Tissue," explains the mind-body symptoms caused by traumatic bonding. Victims of TBRs feel shame, emotional pain, loss of self, and cognitive dissonance. I will explain these symptoms, how they occur, and why they cause the victim to stay bonded.

Chapter 6, "Getting off the Merry-Go-Round of Insanity," describes how women wake up and leave trauma bonds. It is a loss of safety for some women; others emotionally detach from their partners. Some women become more confident and feel strong enough to leave. And some get discarded by their abuser.

Chapter 7, "How to Leave Safely," explains just that: how to get out of a trauma bond carefully and with the least amount of damage possible.

Part 3, "The Wisdom of the Wound," is about how you can recover emotionally once you've left.

Chapter 8, "Post-Traumatic Growth," demonstrates that finding meaning is not the same as saying, "All things happen for a reason." Meaning comes from actively confronting yourself, learning from your mistakes, and being open to change.

Chapter 9, "Avoiding the Future PL," explains how to never again get into another trauma bond with a pathological lover (PL) when you're ready to begin dating again.

Chapter 10, "Go Live," concludes the book with the idea that you can heal and learn from your trauma bond, going on to enjoy healthy relationships in the future.

As you read this book, keep in mind that resilience does not mean being invulnerable, but rather you are inviolable. Because you can no longer be violated, you can handle life's inevitable challenges. Your recovery and growth are the goals.

Trauma bonds are life-altering but do not have to be a life sentence. I am living proof that you can grow from a trauma bond. Post-traumatic growth (PTG) research confirms that most trauma bond victims develop enhanced personal strength and become open to new possibilities as they recover. Seventy-five percent of people who experience such trauma grow from it.[5] I don't know about you, but I think that's an encouraging statistic that people should know!

After recovering from a trauma bond, you can improve psychological well-being, experience a positive personality change, and develop healthy coping mechanisms leading to constructive changes such as self-love and healthy intimacy. I have seen this play out again and again in my therapy room and beyond. So, are you ready to commit to your personal growth and recovery? Turn the page if you believe you are worth it. I know you are.

PART 1

Dangerously in Love

1 What Your Mother Never Told You

> There are unique qualities when the trauma is by the hand of
> those who are supposed to love, protect, and cherish us.[1]
>
> **—PATRICK CARNES**

WE ARE OBSESSED WITH LOVE. But what do we truly understand about the act of loving? According to Erich Fromm, "Love is an art that requires knowledge and effort, and it is the active concern for the life and growth of that which we love."[2] It sounds simple, yet sharing love is a mystery. Seventy-five percent of my patients come to therapy because they are devastated by heartbreak, divorce, or relationship betrayal. One of the most common themes I've heard as a therapist is a big gap between "the intimacy I long for and the romantic love I have experienced." These adults want a different intimate encounter—perhaps this is a sentiment you are experiencing now.

Our deepest longings and most tender needs come to life in romantic love. Intimacy is the daring plunge into a physical and emotional connection. As euphoric as a passionate bond feels, it can cause just as much agony. The terms *intimate relationships* or *intimate partners* are used throughout this book to be inclusive of any romantic and sexual relationship between two non-biologically related people, including dating or marital relationships, relationships in which the romantic partners cohabitate, and relationships in which two people have children in common yet are no longer romantically or sexually involved with one another.

Ideally, loving relationships are supportive, protective, and safe for each couple member. Unfortunately, some connections can devolve into abusive attachments called trauma bonds. Trauma bonding is the process of emotionally attaching to a lover who is mean and controlling, yet their partner stays loyal to them despite the pain.[3] Abuse may end when a relationship ends. However, in trauma bonds, abuse often continues or worsens once a relationship is over.

Trauma bonds are a growing pain for millions of women. The COVID-19 pandemic alone has increased domestic violence by 8 percent.[4] Modern society confirms physical violence as credible, verifiable, or legitimate abuse. In the United States, nearly twenty people per minute—equaling 1,200 an hour, 28,800 daily, and 10 million people yearly—are victims of family and domestic violence.[5] And one in four American women experience intimate partner violence (IPV) from their trusted lovers annually.[6] And I cannot give you the exact number of women because our health organizations are only starting to recognize coercive control and verbal abuse as actual abuse. Even more concerning is that nonviolent abuse is equally or more harmful than physical abuse.[7]

Much psychological research exists on victims and abusers in trauma bonds. Previously, the domestic violence community focused on physical and sexual abuse. However, researchers in intimate partner abuse (IPA) are now interested in psychological abuse, including nonphysical behaviors the abuser uses to control, isolate, or intimidate their lover. Often, the abuser in a trauma bond uses a combination of manipulative brainwashing and psychological bullying to break down their partner's self-esteem, creating emotional dependency and making it feel impossible to leave. Coercive control, or pressuring a partner, is a form of emotional abuse and plays a significant role in trauma bonds.[8]

The weapons of coercive control are deception, exploitation, isolation, and intimidation, and they are mainly invisible to others.[9] Abusers use such behaviors to maintain power and control without potentially subjecting themselves to trouble with the law. That's why this type of control is so insidious. Yet, if you can name and know the tactics of coercive control, you have taken an essential step toward eliminating them in your life.

Traumatic bonding can look different depending on the relationship. Still, TBRs need to have two main characteristics: intermittent abuse and a power imbalance, which create the conditions for traumatic bonding to occur.

INTERMITTENT ABUSE

Traumatic bonding is a mystery to many people because they wonder why on earth a woman could stay with a man and be so seemingly immune to his abuse. The answer is a behavioral cycle called *intermittent reinforcement*. Intermittent reinforcement is the repeated cycle of one partner betraying, harming, and then loving their partner. Traumatic bonding occurs when one partner has an abusive behavior pattern, causing their lover to feel fearful. The abuse leaves the woman drained, afraid, and desperate for support or care. Therefore, she will likely soak in her abuser's promises that he will never hurt her again and his pledges of eternal love after the cruelty.

Have you been in this cycle? Do you know someone who has?

The enormous change between extremely caring gestures and intense aggression creates an emotional attachment between the two partners that intensifies this unhealthy bond. The abuser's lack of predictability and uncontrollability are glue-like elements that seal the connection between these two people. Research on animal learning demonstrated how animals trained with a mixture of love and violence became 230 percent more attached to their trainers than when the animals were exposed to consistent love.[10] Actually, it's the extremity of both the cruelty and kindness that intensifies the bond. Yikes! Also, periodic episodes of mistreatment create space and time for the victim to reconnect with their partner emotionally.

For example, a man becomes verbally explosive and emotionally abusive out of nowhere and says to his girlfriend, "You're a bitch. No wonder your last boyfriend couldn't stand the sight of you and left your ass." Yet when the same man thinks he's losing his girlfriend, he switches gears and becomes apologetic and loving. However, his apologies lack true accountability or genuine remorse for the pain his nasty insults cause the woman he claims to love.

This abuse creates a longing in the victim for kindness and relief from feeling hurt and afraid. Desperate for relief, the victim perceives any person who can soothe them as a rescuer. Because abuse is so entangled with shame, she doesn't tell anyone. So, this leaves her open to only being soothed by her abuser. In traumatic bonding, the person who offers comfort is the same one who terrorizes.

Does this sound familiar?

One moment of connection is a positive reinforcer for many victims. The belief that he will change, things will get better, and the pain will stop is a powerful stimulant of hope for women. Intermittent reinforcement creates enough hope to tolerate the emotional pain and suffering that occupy most of her time in this trauma bond. His manipulation of hopefulness is also a means to ensure her dependence by encouraging her desire to please him. Traumatically bonded women confuse intense mixes of abuse and manipulation with love.

That's why it can be so hard to leave.

A POWER IMBALANCE

A major imbalance of power fuels trauma bonds, which is another reason why it can be so hard to leave. According to social power theory, power is defined by a person's ability to control or influence another person.[11] The person with the most resources and decision-making ability has the most power. The decision power index assesses who has the final say in six issues: buying a car, having children, what apartment to take, what job either partner should take, whether a partner should work, and how much money to spend each week on food.

However, a person doesn't simply have power because they have resources and make the most decisions. They have power because their lover *needs* or *depends* on those resources. So, in a relationship, the more dependent you are on your lover, the more invested you are. This includes emotional dependency, which can be the most intense need of all.

As a result of the abuser's desperate need for power and control, they will exploit their partner's trust and love. Criticism, isolation, threats, and sometimes even physical violence are the weapons of coercive control these abusers use to dominate their victims. These abusers will use manipulative brainwashing strategies such as gaslighting, lying, and exploitation against their intimate partners. The abusive partner can also use psychological violence to intentionally harm their lover by degrading, micromanaging, stalking, sexually coercing, belittling, exploiting, or punishing them.

Therefore, even if the relationship starts with both partners feeling equal, over time, the abuser's dominating behaviors instill fear in their lover, and the power dynamics shift. The balance of power diminishes, with the abuser gaining more power and the ability to control their lover.[12]

A relationship you'd hoped would involve loving support ends up being a trap designed for domination. As a result, a victim feels anxious, dependent, and afraid, deprived of independence, self-esteem, and fundamental rights.

Controlling another person is at the root of all trauma bonds.

If you or someone you know might be in a trauma bond relationship, take the assessment on page 80 (or online at drnae.com/assessments). If you answer yes to at least eight of the fourteen questions, consider yourself trauma bonded. Good thing you're reading this book.

Four examples of different trauma-bonded couples follow to demonstrate the various ways the two foundational conditions of trauma bonding—intermittent abuse and power imbalance—manifest. I want to acknowledge that reading the stories below can be triggering. Yet I purposely included them because I know you might identify with or see something of your relationship in the scenarios I describe. And I understand how validating that can feel.

However, if you feel emotionally overwhelmed and sense your body tensing or your heart racing, please stop, and take a break. Then revisit the material once you feel calmer. This book is here to educate and support you in healing from traumatic bonding, so please be kind to yourself and take it in at your own pace.

Also, there is a wonderful reciprocal relationship between your emotions and breathing. You can use the simple breathing exercise that follows to self-soothe when difficult emotions and insights emerge. Your breath is a beautiful ally in creating calmness. Your breath is always available, and it's free.

Sit upright while relaxing your body. With your mouth closed, inhale for a count of four. Open your mouth as you slowly exhale for a count of six. To soothe your nervous system, your exhale must be longer than your inhale. Repeat this pattern of conscious breathing three to six times or until you begin to feel calmer.

Keri

Keri, a forty-two-year-old woman, called me because she felt stuck in her career. She had vowed to have better self-care as her New Year's resolution, and personal therapy was a part of that process. Keri was a digital researcher uninspired by her work; she yearned for a more meaningful occupation. She imagined writing screenplays for a streaming channel and wondered how she could do that. In her second session, she briefly mentioned her husband, Nick, a local city official.

Several sessions later, Keri asked if she could bring in her husband for a couple's session. It is uncommon for me to switch from individual therapy to couple's therapy. Yet, we agreed it would only be for one session. The next week, Nick strolled into my office behind Keri and gave a charming smile as he complimented my décor. We got right into it, and Nick was calm yet adamant that Keri keep her research career. He said the family relied on her income, especially with the girls going to college soon.

Keri loved Nick deeply, so she accommodated his request and allowed him to have power over her career choice. In my clinical opinion, Keri believed that if she changed jobs without Nick's blessing, she would lose his love. That's because their love was transactional. In therapy, Keri and I discussed that love does not require sacrificing ourselves, our needs, dreams, and desires. Yet, she had convinced herself Nick was right and said it was easier to do what he wanted to keep her marriage peaceful.

In retrospect, Keri probably wanted me to convince Nick that changing careers was the right move to avoid having to assert herself directly and endure his wrath. As I got to know Keri, I realized her career was not the only thing Nick had control over, yet after a few more sessions, she said she felt better and terminated therapy.

A year later, Keri called and asked to resume therapy. When she returned, she had a very different narrative of her marriage. Keri mentioned how her husband went to local bars a few evenings during the week and would frequently come home drunk. When she would confront Nick about his drinking and that she felt ignored, he would punch holes in walls and threaten her with, "If you don't like it, leave. Get a new husband. You can't tell me how to live." His reactions intimidated her, and he continued psychologically bullying Keri into submission to get away with his poor behavior. And it worked.

Keri said he never physically harmed her, yet she did always wonder if the next punch would be to her face. She admitted that sometimes she wished he would hit her, as it would prove his abusiveness. Nights usually ended with him passed out and her crying and cleaning up whatever messes he'd made. The following day, she would wake up to a bright-eyed Nick making her breakfast and asking her if he could do something special, like go to a meditation class with her. Keri would be so relieved to wake up to a happy husband that she'd always say, "Yes!" Nick's acts of kindness and attention worked like anesthesia; they numbed her pain from the night before. This scene illustrates the pattern of cruel, insensitive treatment mixed with random bursts of kindness—the intermittent abuse that is a foundation of a trauma bond. Of course, Nick's kindness was fake; he only used it to manipulate Keri so he could keep living his life of excessive indulgence.

Nick also controlled Keri's activities, acting as a typical male gatekeeper. Nick insisted that Keri always have her phone on so he could track her location—he claimed he wanted to ensure she was safe. Yet, Keri felt smothered by him. And if she wanted to do something fun for herself, like go on a girls' trip for a weekend, Nick would become enraged, convinced she was going because she wanted to cheat on him. This was, of course, a ridiculous scenario to Keri—she would never cheat on her husband—and she wondered why he would even accuse her of that. So, to avoid his violent outbursts, Keri often gave in to Nick's anger, leaving her phone on, skipping out on girls' trips, and even limiting her self-care time and nights out with friends.

Keri was very conscientious, and Nick took advantage of that. In addition to her career, she oversaw all the household chores—cleaning, caring for the dog, paying the bills, and doing the laundry. Her whole life felt like work, inside the house and out. Meanwhile, Nick was out almost every night partying "with colleagues." In our sessions, Keri often said that she didn't know where taking care stopped and taking advantage began.

One day, a tiny voice inside her said, "Look at his phone." Feeling frustrated that Nick was lying about where and who he was with every night, yet unable to confront him directly because of his rageful reactions, Keri scrolled through his phone while he was passed out. She found out Nick was on the Grindr app, which is used to meet homosexual men.

Keri felt emotionally trapped. She said she felt stupid for allowing this to happen and blamed herself. However, she could not contain her rage and unleashed her wrath on Nick when he arrived home the next day. When confronted, Nick deflected and screamed, "How could you look through my phone?" Nick flipped the script and became angry, intimidating Keri into saying she was sorry.

Keri then told me in therapy that she felt wrong for not trusting and accusing him of meeting men, even though she had seen undeniable evidence with her own eyes. "What's wrong with me?" she thought, utterly gaslit by years of abuse.

A few weeks later, while sitting at my desk, my phone rang; it was Keri, and she sounded despondent. She said she and Nick had picked up their two daughters from a party the night before, and Aimee and Stella had gotten into a fight in the back of the car. Nick stopped the car, flung open the back door, ripped Stella out, opened the trunk, and threw her in it. Nick drove them all home to the sound of Stella screaming and crying in the trunk. As Keri told me this story, she sounded emotionally detached from its traumatic impact.

Keri was so desensitized to Nick's violence that she had normalized his throwing their daughter into the car's trunk and driving home, even though she witnessed her daughter's pain and her other daughter's utter terror.

I paused, took a breath, and said, "Are you sure you don't want to get a restraining order on Nick?"

She said, "I need to think about that. Restraining orders are profound."

I replied, "Physical violence of that extreme nature, such as tossing your daughter into the trunk of your car, is serious. The decision is yours. I trust you will decide what's right for you. Yet as a licensed therapist, I will have to report Nick's behaviors to Child Protective Services."

Thank goodness, something inside Keri snapped that day, and she finally realized her husband was dangerous!

Nick was psychologically savvy; he had a good mixture of charm and indignant outrage sprinkled with deflective threats. Keri's husband was also a controlling, pathological liar who used her as a housekeeper, abused her and her daughters, and was a rageful alcoholic. Once Keri recognized her daughters were physically unsafe, she woke up.

Keri decided not to file a restraining order, yet she served Nick with divorce papers. He did not fight their separation and proceeded to move in with one of his lovers. Nick, of course, left Keri in charge of selling their home and moving the girls out.

An unspoken fact about TBRs is their ripple effect on children's development. Research shows that children who have witnessed physical violence have a higher incidence of assaulting their mothers and siblings.[13] Even though Keri left Nick, she now had to deal with Aimee's verbal abuse toward her and Stella. Aimee exhibited the same threatening, dominating behaviors as Nick. When Keri tried to parent Aimee and set boundaries, she would scream, "You can't tell me what to do!" and repeatedly hit Keri. Aimee's outbursts happened weekly and made it hard for Keri to build a new personal life, as her attention was focused on her abusive daughter. You can get rid of an abusive partner but not an abusive child.

The other daughter, Stella, had developed an eating disorder and required hospitalization. Keri dealt with her girls' emotional issues by herself and with the help of several therapists. Nick, of course, was checked out, living his best life with his new girlfriend/victim, not taking any accountability for the wreckage that his behavior had caused his family. As Keri endured their trauma bond's effect on her daughters, she worked through the guilt she felt for staying with Nick for so long. And she wondered if she and her daughters would ever truly recover from the effects of his abuse, lies, and cruelty. Several years later, Keri, Aimee, and Stella continue trying to heal as a family.

Lily

Lily was a childhood friend of my niece who came to therapy seeking help in her relationship. A driven, intelligent, extroverted young woman in her twenties, Lily skillfully hid an upbringing filled with abuse by wearing a mask of perfection and achievement. Lily had grown up witnessing and enduring her parents' trauma-bonded marriage. She has been in several toxic relationships herself, though she could not understand why she continued falling for deceitful partners. On the outside, Lily seemed to have everything going for her: she was a straight-A student, held numerous leadership positions outside of school, was hardworking, belonged to several social circles, and was on the fast track to becoming a therapist herself. Yet on the inside, Lily felt disconnected, tired, and lonely.

Lily explained how life became much more exciting when she began dating Jason, someone she met at a bar one fateful night. He was eight years older than her and was a fun-loving, charming, athletic guy with a mysterious but playful edge that Lily enjoyed. On their first date, Lily shared that she was pursuing a career as a therapist, and he disclosed that he went to therapy every week. Bingo! She was hooked. The two saw each other almost daily for the first several weeks, and he showered her with texts, attention, remarks of self-awareness, and vulnerability. He told her about his upbringing—the heartache of his father's very early death, then losing his stepfather to alcoholism, and consoling his grieving mother through it all. He shared stories about his childhood abuse and failed relationships and how therapy helped him overcome so much. Lily felt that he could understand the pain she had buried deep down. Her loneliness eased as she began to merge with him.

In the beginning, Lily recounted endlessly fun weekends spent going on dates, meeting his beloved mom and group of friends, exploring new parts of the city, having great sex, and going to concerts. Jason was a music fanatic and introduced her to the party drug Molly, which slowly became a regular part of their weekend routines, especially at shows. Then, as quickly as the love bombing had begun, it fizzled out. Lily chalked it up to the countless wild nights they had spent doing coke, Molly, and mushrooms while partying into the early morning. Jason's exciting lifestyle caught up to her, and she struggled to keep up. Still, she was emotionally hooked and determined to figure it out with him.

Conversations with Jason became strained; Lily had difficulty getting past the walls he suddenly had up. He would only let them down when drugs or alcohol were involved, which motivated her to continue colluding with his substance-fueled lifestyle. The two began fighting more often, Jason stopped taking the initiative in planning their dates, and they rarely had sex anymore. When they did, Lily felt awkward and blamed her insecurities and extensive history of sexual trauma.

One day, a small voice told Lily to look through Jason's phone. She had noticed his protectiveness over it; it was always in his pocket, even when they were at home lounging around. Following a surprisingly pleasant morning together, Jason offered to cook breakfast and left his phone by the bed without realizing it. Lily jumped at the opportunity, having planned precisely how she would search through the phone quickly. She opened his Snapchat and found an exchange of messages and nude images between Jason and another woman. She also noticed a dating app. Lily froze. Just then, Jason walked in.

"What the fuck are you doing with my phone?" he shouted.

"What the fuck are you doing?" she asked through her tears, telling him about the nude photos and dating app she'd seen. The two shouted at the top of their lungs for twenty minutes before Lily gathered her things and stormed out.

Within two weeks, Jason convinced Lily to meet him for coffee. In the meantime, he sent manipulative texts masked as heartfelt sincerity and regret. Jason was open, honest, vulnerable, and highly communicative when she met him for coffee. A conversation ensued, and he revealed painful details about his past: sexual abuse by an older cousin in childhood, a history of dating abusive women who criticized him when he couldn't perform sexually, a hidden porn addiction, deep insecurities, and a strong need for validation, which he got from the dating apps. Jason justified his hurtful actions and admitted that his substance use filled his need for another dopamine hit to relieve the pain he felt every day. His psychobabble seduced Lily. His vulnerability pulled at Lily's heart, and she thought, "I can handle this. My love and loyalty will make him change."

Nearly six months later, Jason's smoke screen finally came crashing down. After an afternoon filled with sunshine and sangria, Jason fell asleep while the two watched TV. His phone had fallen between the sofa cushions. Without hesitation, Lily grabbed it and slipped into the bedroom. He was out cold, making the opportunity golden. It took her about an hour to piece together the intricate web of lies he had constructed since their relationship started. Lily found that Jason was actively sleeping with twenty-five other girls, was on dating apps (including Grindr), and had been using drugs (including cocaine) and alcohol almost every night. As she dug deeper, she saw he had a long history of late-night Uber receipts to countless homes and a record of frequent Venmo payments for sexual encounters; the most recent visit to a sex worker was just hours before he'd come over that day. She also found graphic sexual images in text exchanges with numerous unsaved numbers and a folder of vivid nude photos and videos buried in his phone.

In this golden hour, Lily learned of Jason's secret life. Her two years of gut feelings and rightful anxiety were instantly validated, and a wave of relief washed over her for the first time in a long time. She felt a clear and absolute certainty that she was done for good.

She then woke him up and said, "Jason, I know all of it, every bit. Tell me that you at least used protection." He tried to lash out in anger, but she stopped him.

"Here's your phone. Get out of my house. I'm done. I hope you find the help you need and whatever it is you want." After that night, she blocked him on all fronts and never spoke to him again, though he did find ways to contact her.

Lily and Jason's relationship had followed a pattern of manipulation, deceit, blowups, breakups, and makeups for two years. All in all, the two broke up and got back together seven or eight times. Each betrayal felt like a laceration to Lily's heart, and every time, Jason preyed on her Achilles' heel of vulnerability. He preyed on her desperation to feel love.

Thankfully, Lily was able to pull herself out of her trauma bond and found a therapist who was equipped to handle her painful history. She continues excelling in school and has been in a healthy and healing relationship for two years.

Alex

Alex was a young woman in her thirties. She was pregnant and had been married for two years to a handsome stockbroker who was "a genius with numbers." The two met on a blind date, and Alex described their meeting as "love at first sight." Tom had been married to a horrible woman who lied and cheated on him; Alex had a similar ex-partner, so they empathized with each other. As time passed and the two dated,

Tom told Alex her love "brought hope to him that there are good women in the world." Tom's wounds were apparent, and Alex hid hers by staying busy and focused on other people. She wanted to make his happiness and success her project.

Six months after the meeting, they married, but things quickly worsened. During their first year of marriage, Tom became incredibly controlling, wanting Alex's life to revolve around him more and more. She described it as living in prison. Tom made a list of people with whom Alex could hang out, and Alex initially thought it was because Tom loved her deeply and only wanted the best for her. After all, you are whom you surround yourself with. Even though she obliged, Alex felt strange about it. She felt erased.

Initially, Alex was a highly paid account executive at an advertising agency. But after the two married, Tom demanded she quit her job as they did not need the money. When Alex pushed back, claiming that she liked her career and the self-esteem it gave her, Tom gave her the silent treatment for a week. Tom knew that his refusal to connect with her felt like a slow death. She finally quit her job so that he would speak to her again. Ignoring another person is not the absence of communication—it is a vital communication of power.

In therapy, Alex described the high cost of living with Tom: "I gave up my life for him. I lost my career and friends, gave up on my dreams, and even distanced myself from my family. Everything revolves around him and his needs, and I'm expected to bend backward for him. He can never compromise, and my needs never matter. I've done everything possible to be seen as valuable in his eyes, but I'm never enough!"

Alex explained how Tom was super possessive and jealous. One afternoon, he saw that Alex had commented on an old boyfriend's Instagram post. He got angry with her, yelled, screamed, and even wrestled Alex to the floor. Alex was embarrassed about what she'd done and how Tom had treated her.

Alex described what it was like to be pregnant with Tom as her husband. He was always angry at her. At thirty-six weeks, Alex had a terrible stomach virus that caused her to vomit continually. Four days into her sickness, she saw blood in her vomit. She was alarmed and screamed for Tom to take her to the doctor. Tom casually replied, "Alex, please let me blow-dry my hair first." His needs were always more important than hers. Luckily, Alex was fine, and three weeks later, she gave birth to a beautiful girl.

Motherhood agreed with Alex, but fatherhood did not agree with Tom. He was moody all the time once the baby was born. Alex believed that Tom was jealous of the attention and affection she bestowed upon their newborn. Then, Tom began staying out later and later for client dinners and suddenly had to travel more.

When he was home, Tom's verbal abuse increased. He told Alex she was fat and would never lose the baby weight, and how could he be attracted to her when she looked so tired and out of shape? Alex tried to please Tom any way she could; she kept a lovely home, did home work-outs while the baby slept, was a good mother, and did everything Tom asked of her during the day. Even then, Alex recalled that nothing she did was enough, and Tom's mood swings continued evolving. He could be in the worst mood, but a business call would come through, and he would suddenly perk up and behave happily. The second he got off his business call, he would go back to ignoring her or throwing a tantrum. Alex said, "I felt like a turtle dying in my shell."

When I asked Alex to reflect on how she might have contributed to their toxic dynamic, she admitted, "I'm a people pleaser, and I always have been. Disappointing anyone I love or value hurts more than any punishment anyone could give me. I'd do almost anything to avoid that discomfort. I sacrifice pieces of myself, my needs, well-being, or happiness, and I do this with Tom. Deep down, I believe I can earn his love if I'm good enough, and maybe he'll finally treat me well if I'm perfect in every way."

As a therapist, it is not my job to tell my patients what to do or when to leave traumatic bonding. I ensure they are safe and support them wherever they need until they are ready.

One day, Alex texted me and explained that while on vacation with Tom, his abuse escalated with constant insults and accusations that she was stealing from him, and he tried to strangle her after a fight. His domination was escalating. She was scared for her physical safety and financial security, so we devised a plan. I suggested that she let a friend know that Tom had become abusive and for her to text that friend to call the police when he laid a hand on her.

Sure enough, one night, Tom came home drunk, and he tried to choke her again. She texted her friend, and fifteen minutes later, the police arrived, separated them, and questioned them. The police sent an emergency order to the judge, and Alex got a five-day restraining order. Then her attorney got a twenty-one-day restraining order. After the court held a permanent hearing, she got an eighteen-month restraining order. Tom could not contact, intimidate, or threaten Alex directly or through a third party. Tom was required to stay away from Alex's home and could never come within one hundred feet of her.

He could only have supervised visits once a week for two hours with their young child. However, like many trauma-bonded relationships, the abuse continued, despite their not living together. Tom was furious that Alex now had the upper hand and that he could no longer control her. Tom denied the abuse and never paid child support on time. The court ordered them not to touch their bank accounts, but Tom ignored that and depleted their mutual savings account.

Tom harassed the child's visitation monitor to demand more time with their daughter. He violated the restraining order by asking his mother to text Alex constantly, insisting that she see her granddaughter. Tom called all their mutual friends and started a smear campaign saying that Alex stole money, which was why he was physically abusive.

Yet, because Alex was committed to her personal growth, she worked diligently in therapy, hired an attorney specializing in high-conflict divorce, and stuck to the strategies suggested by her divorce coach. She resourced herself as much as possible to fight for her and her daughter's well-being and safety. While she still has moments of pain, this pain is constructive, unlike the destructive suffering she experienced with Tom.

Juno

Juno came to see me after an intense trauma-bonded marriage ended, which had left her depressed, anxious, and lonely. She had met her ex-husband, Larry, on Bumble after she moved out from living with a roommate who bullied her. After their first date, Larry gave Juno overwhelming attention, dropping by daily with substantial flower bouquets—especially tulips, her favorite. Larry gave her countless gifts, fixed things around Juno's new house, and bought food for her cat. He would constantly text throughout the day and continued doing so even after Juno asked him to stop because she was training for her new job and his texts were distracting. She bonded with Larry even more when she discovered they had both gotten sober a few months before they met, leading Juno to feel that Larry was her soulmate.

Juno explained that Larry had a gambling problem at the beginning of their relationship. Yet, Larry claimed he was so in love with Juno that she kept him on the straight and narrow, and he did not want to gamble anymore. He even left the therapist he saw for the gambling problem and stopped going to Gamblers Anonymous meetings because of Juno's love. He convinced Juno to quit her well-paying job so he could take care of her for the "rest of her life." Juno recalled feeling so secure in Larry's love for her because of his adoration and the fact that he claimed he needed her.

Yet one thing felt rather bizarre to Juno: right before she and Larry had met, his parents died in a fatal car accident. Larry hadn't seemed troubled by this, and Juno questioned Larry about his lack of grief. She was surprised he did not express any emotion about their sudden death, even though he claimed to love them deeply. She wondered how he could be so emotionally disconnected.

In therapy, Juno explained that she discovered Larry was having an affair fifteen years into their relationship. She had a gut feeling and followed him after he left the house one day. Sure enough, Larry went straight to a local motel. Juno waited in her parked car, and two hours later, he opened the hotel room door and emerged with a woman. Juno got out of her vehicle and confronted Larry in the parking lot. The woman quickly ran to her car and sped away. Juno felt devastated by Larry's betrayal and wanted to leave him, yet he threatened suicide, and she pitied him. Larry's demands were both unpredictable and unrelenting.

Later, Larry blamed Juno for his cheating. He claimed they were in a "dead marriage before the affair." Deep down, Juno thought she deserved his unloving behavior. Then he would flip the script, cry, apologize for what he'd said, and beg her forgiveness. His gestures of caring mixed with betrayal intensified their bond. She wanted more out of life but felt paralyzed by her fear of being alone. Larry's behavior left her feeling trapped and powerless, and she suffered constant brain fog and emotional confusion, so she stayed.

Juno needed to calm her nerves and escape the pain of Larry's cheating and gaslighting, so she started drinking again and mixing alcohol with Xanax. She needed to block the trauma of their relationship. After some time, Larry began drinking again as well. One night, he came home aggravated and had a few martinis to ease his stress. Juno joined him, thinking maybe the alcohol would help them enjoy a night together. After a few drinks, she tried to initiate sex with her husband, but he began criticizing her body. "You've gained too much weight since you started drinking again. I don't want to fuck you when you look like this! If you don't lose all that weight, I will have to find someone else." He pushed her off him, and she tumbled onto the floor. Towering over her, Larry continued taunting Juno as she sobbed and felt helpless. When she got up, he charged at her, but she shoved him away and called the police.

The police separated Larry and Juno, but Juno was afraid and embarrassed to tell the police the truth. She was also scared that if Larry got arrested for domestic violence, he could lose his job, and she would lose her financial security. So, she lied and said nothing had happened. She told the police Larry was stressed out, yet she started the fight, it was her fault, and it was a mistake to call them. Yet, in the other room, Larry said Juno had hit him first and feared for his safety. The police cuffed Juno and got an emergency order from the judge for a five-day restraining order. Juno was shocked and screamed at the police, "This is wrong! Stop! He's lying!" Her blood-curdling screams were only further proof that she was the crazy one.

Juno spent four nights in jail, thinking for sure Larry would bail her out. She kept calling and texting Larry, pleading with him to bring her some clothes and toiletries. He never called her back and never went to get her. When she realized he would never respond, she called her sister, who bailed her out. Yet, while Juno was in jail, Larry got a lawyer to extend the restraining order against her. He also used character blackmail and tried to "pull" her family and friends away from Juno to create an even more profound sense of emotional and social isolation from life.

The next time Juno was face-to-face with Larry was in court. Larry used the voicemails that Juno sent him from jail to show the judge that she was dangerous to him as she broke the restraining order by contacting him. Juno was charged with domestic battery, which is a misdemeanor. The restraining order protecting Larry from her was granted for a year. She got a year of probation as this was her first offense. Larry suggested that Juno go to rehab as it would look good to the judge, and she listened to him as she saw how ruthless he was.

Larry sent clothes to the hotel that Juno was staying in before she went off to rehab for three months. He changed the locks on their house and removed her name from their cars. After Juno left the drug rehab, she lived in a sober house. She currently resides in an apartment and is working as a schoolteacher. She was traumatized and heartbroken by Larry's ruthless betrayals. Yet, she realizes that she depended on Larry for her identity, self-esteem, and security. Her agreeable nature and overdependency, combined with Larry's selfishness, deception, and lack of remorse, sacrificed Juno's well-being. But she is now on the road to recovery.

As these tragic stories reveal, trauma bonding induces extensive physical, emotional, and relational harm to partners and children. Over time, women—perhaps even you—have become their lover's safety blanket and punching bag. The woman's *hook* is *hope* for true love. What type of person promises to love and trust and then is cruel, deceptive, and controlling? The next chapter describes in more detail this intimate terrorist.

KEY POINTS TO REMEMBER

1. Nonviolent abuse is equally or more harmful than physical abuse.

2. A trauma bond does not need to feature blatant physical abuse; the abuser in a trauma bond uses a combination of manipulation, psychological bullying, and coercive control (deception, exploitation, isolation, and intimidation) to break down their partner's self-esteem to create emotional dependency.

3. Traumatic bonding is a relational process that requires the conditions of intermittent abuse and a power imbalance.

4. Intermittent reinforcement is the repeated cycle of one partner betraying, harming, and then loving their partner. The fluctuation

between caring gestures and emotional aggression forms the glue that intensifies this unhealthy bond.

5. Power is a person's ability to control or influence another person. One has power because their lover *needs or depends* on those resources. The more dependent a person is, including emotional dependency, the more they are invested in the relationship, the more abuse they tolerate, and the harder they fight to stay. Also, the abuser in a trauma bond gains power over time by instilling fear in his lover through his dominating behavior.

2 Is He Twisted or Tender?

> When a man who wants no commitment behaves like a
> passionate suitor, he gives off a set of mixed messages, a
> simultaneous flashing of red and green lights.[1]
>
> **—PETER TRACHTENBERG**

ALL PEOPLE HAVE PERSONALITIES AND personality styles. We might say that someone is moody or antisocial, but a person's character is more complex than a list of adjectives; it includes people's patterns of thoughts, feelings, and behaviors that distinguish them from others. Our personality results from genetics and environmental forces, such as family, upbringing, and culture.[2] It is perhaps what we are most aware of when we are intimately connected.

As you've undoubtedly experienced, your lover's personality affects the quality of your relationship. When you intend to love and care for your partner genuinely, you are motivated to understand them. You are curious about their behaviors, thoughts, and feelings. You can also reflect on how your behavior impacts your lover.

If you are a person with a moral compass, you live by prosocial values and possess the capacity to be honest. As a balanced person, you can recognize your uniqueness and can differentiate between yourself and others. If you feel secure, you can be vulnerable and authentic. Thus, you can be tender and truthful in intimacy.

This does *not* describe a trauma bond abuser.

So, let's dive into the TBR perpetrator's personality. If you can learn what makes them tick, you can hopefully avoid them in the future or help someone else you know and love to avoid entering a trauma bond.

A quick note before we jump into the deep end: This chapter can be challenging to read—even for me! Yet it contains a wealth of crucial, research-based data. So, take your time, process the information, and be gentle with yourself. Many women want to know "why," and this chapter explores some of those answers. It's a necessary but often difficult step.

THE PATHOLOGICAL LOVER

Why do some men criticize, dominate, and physically harm women with whom they are intimately involved? An abusive male's pathological personality fuels the toxic dynamics of a trauma bond—"pathological" means suffering from a mental disease. I will use "pathological lover" (PL) to name the perpetrator in a TBR because anyone who can continually lie and abuse others in the name of love is mentally unwell.

If you're reading this, you already know that a pathological, controlling partner is ruthlessly self-centered. His identity is tied to the amount of money, power, and attention he can attain and the pleasure he can feel. His needs come first, and this belief drives his conduct. Power protects him from the harsh realities of being human. Humanness is alien to a pathological person. He can be a hero or invisible, but nothing in between. The in-between is to be human, which is to accept one's helplessness in life, recognize one's dependence on others, and admit one's failures and vulnerabilities. The PL's primary tool for being in a relationship is coercive control because it assures him all the cozy comforts of owning his lover.

PLs are selfish con artists who initially charm and intentionally harm you without remorse. A PL uses aggressive intimidation, often saying, "Don't you dare say that or else!" or manipulation such as, "How on earth could I have cheated? I texted you that night to let you know where I was." Psychological threats and manipulative lies are fueled by their belief that they are superior to you. Therefore, they think they have a right to exploit your trust and love. Distorted views and no moral compass feed their entitlement and make them feel unstoppable.[3]

PLs have a diverse toolbox of infidelity. The PL has a perpetual desire for sexual excitement, which causes them to betray their partners continually; they think tenderness and loyalty are for fools. Infidelity is any behavior that violates an agreement between two people with a sexual, romantic bond. Infidelity isn't just physical intimacy; in today's digital age, it could be sexting, becoming emotionally invested with someone else, or using dating apps while in a current romantic relationship. For this book, infidelity is the betrayal of the couple's stated commitment of intimate exclusivity without the other partner's consent.

Unfortunately, trusting, good-natured women are easily seduced by the PL's charismatic mask, which he explicitly curates to hide his insensitive, narcissistic personality. If you suspect you are currently in a trauma bond, I hope the following sections provide insight into the darkness of your partner's true personality and inspire you to leave. If you have already survived a TBR, I hope the information that follows helps you identify and avoid a PL in the future. Regardless, I am confident this information will inspire self-compassion for your pain and validation for what you have lived through. Yet most importantly, it will provide education, so you are *never* tricked into falling in love with a pathological person again.

Cluster B Personality Disorders

PLs' complex personalities make them hard to figure out. It took me a master's, a PhD, and over a decade of dedication to relational trauma research to decode this lethal lover. It's no wonder you never saw him coming! So, let's unpack their personalities. No doubt many of these attributes will be familiar to you.

According to Sandra L. Brown, MA, in her seminal book *Women Who Love Psychopaths*, the PL has what is clinically classified as a Cluster B personality disorder (PD).[4] Cluster B PDs are characterized by dramatic, overly emotional, or unpredictable thinking and behaviors that cause issues in work and love. Cluster B disorders include **antisocial personality disorder (ASPD), narcissistic personality disorder (NPD), borderline personality disorder (BPD),** and **histrionic personality disorder (HPD).** These four disorders are grouped due to an overlap in symptoms and presentations. Yet, in this book, I am focusing primarily on personality traits related to ASPD and NPD.

Personality disorders don't affect only the people who have them; they also impact those who love them, work with or for them, or must deal with them regularly. In this book, we'll focus on those who love them. Intimacy is the desire and capacity to develop a close connection with a lover. It is the ability to maintain a romantic relationship by accepting, validating, and respecting your partner. Healthy people yearn for intimacy and fall in love with the hope of authentically bonding with their one true love. Opening yourself up to love gives your partner access to your heart, mind, soul, and life. The very nature of love makes you vulnerable; it is impossible to have love without vulnerability. Without love, human life would have no meaning, as our minds and bodies are wired for connection.

Loving a partner with a Cluster B personality disorder can be traumatizing. A significant other with a Cluster B disorder is selfish; personal gratification, not intimacy, directs their desires. A PL has an erratic way of loving with unpredictable cycles of tenderness and abuse that wound and confuse their partner. Such partners are notoriously greedy and manipulate their lovers to get what they want when they want it.

ASPD and NPD men are as shallow as a puddle; they remain emotionally detached despite dramatic displays of affection. These self-absorbed lovers are not genuinely interested in their partner's lives because relationships are only a means to an end. Cluster B men use cruelty to control their lovers. After they hurt their lovers, they do not feel one drop of remorse. For women who are not PLs, these characteristics are foreign to us. This is a big reason why we don't see them coming or understand their actions and reactions. We expect them to act and react like "normal" people. But they can't; it's not in their personality.

Of course, not even the healthiest relationship is sunshine and rainbows. We all occasionally upset our intimate partners. Adults with certain kinds of personality disorders, however, repeatedly say they will change after causing you distress, yet they don't. You are not unique; they literally and figuratively screw everyone. A PL only presents with a stable personality when you first meet them. It's all part of their charming mask.

THE FIVE-FACTOR PERSONALITY MODEL

As this chapter continues, I have used information gleaned from the five-factor model (FFM) to further explain a PL's character. I use the FFM not only because it is the most scientifically valid measure of personality, but also because, later in the book, I employ this theory to describe women's personalities. Research that stays in the ivory tower does us no good, so I want to tell you what psychological researchers know about the PL's personality.

Universal personality traits exist across cultures, genders, and sexual orientations. PLs have universal personality traits that explain why they traumatize their lovers.

The FFM, also called the Big Five, is a universal tool used to measure personality. One popular assessment has 240 questions and was developed to define as much variety as possible in individuals' personalities using only five categories of traits. Many personality psychologists agree that the five categories capture the most essential, universal, and fundamental individual differences in personality traits.

The five traits are **openness, conscientiousness, extraversion, agreeableness,** and **neuroticism.** Using those traits, we can assess a PL's personality. I won't go into the specific research details of FFM here, but the descriptions of the PLs that follow are based on established scientific FFM findings.[5]

ANTISOCIAL PERSONALITY DISORDER

People with ASPD have a criminal mind because they lack an internal moral compass. They easily violate their lovers' rights and never feel ashamed for emotionally robbing them with deceit and manipulation. Personal gratification is all these social piranhas care about. Intimacy is impossible due to their constant coercion and hostile antagonism. If they think you have harmed them, they will seek and get revenge at all costs. And, like an actual criminal, they strike when you least expect it. Simon Leviev from *The Tinder Swindler*[6] is an example of a person with antisocial personality traits, as he can steal from and manipulate a lover and lie to their face about it.

NARCISSISTIC PERSONALITY DISORDER

Narcissism is a dangerous weed in the garden of personality. Beneath that grandiose, charming mask is a man who is driven by ego, so projecting an excellent image is their primary goal. They are shameless self-promoters and excel at managing first impressions. Admiration is their objective because it gives them power over others. And a relationship with a narcissistic person is transactional as they only care about you if you can help them achieve their goals.

Individuals with NPD struggle to be suitable lovers due to their self-centered need for status and lack of empathy. Narcissism can be divided into two subtypes: grandiose (overt, obvious) and vulnerable (covert, subtle). These subtypes are both associated with exploiting others, low empathy, and antagonism, yet they have differences.[7]

Grandiose Narcissism

Grandiose narcissism (GN) is characterized by feelings of superiority, entitlement, a need for admiration, and self-enhancement strategies. People with GN present as self-absorbed, fearless, bold masters of the universe. Women initially feel safe with them due to their mask of fantasticalness and confidence. However, love is unsustainable with a narcissist.

When falling in love with them, a GN will strike when their lover's idealization of them is hot, allowing them to mold their lover into a dependent and submissive tool. And as the relationship unfolds, it's as if you signed the following contract: "I will let you use all my talents and feed on my heart, and if my contribution doesn't make you shine brighter or doesn't serve your needs, I agree to be devalued, cut down, and discarded as worthless." A relationship with a narcissistic person is transactional. They only care about you if you can help them achieve their goals.

Individuals with GN are "disagreeable extroverts." In public, they are the life of the party, but behind closed doors, they are mean manipulators. Their vain belief that "I am better, so I deserve more" allows them to exploit even the people who love them the most. And God forbid you try to set a boundary or express a need. Then, their tsunami of rage crushes you. Yet, when they are initially seducing you, you feel cherished and pampered.

GNs will aggressively strive to be special, seek admiration, and be better or more successful than others. They will use high-pressure sales tactics to win over their love interest or make a deal happen. GNs will act or exert power to get what they want.

As you might recall, Alex's husband, Tom, had many traits of grandiose narcissism. Tom was an attractive, charismatic, and powerful man who was respected in his community. Everyone at work admired his brash cockiness and ability to make the most complex financial deals work. No one and nothing could get in his way once he put his mind to a task. And at home, he behaved the same. For example, he wanted Alex to be a stay-at-home mom, and since Alex's income was less than his, he forced her to quit. Tom frequently let Alex know that she and their child were financially dependent on him so that he could control her. Tom was the master of their universe, and it was his way or the highway.

GNs seek high excitement and desire admiration from a variety of people. Narcissists have an insatiable need for affection; they can never get enough of it, which is why they cheat and charm relentlessly. Yet admiration is not the same as love. Therefore, GNs are hyperfocused on controlling their partners because they need to know their love source is secure. They require the emotional supply of another's affection to fill their internal emptiness. When one lover's supply is insufficient, GNs set out to charm because they must have their fill, and they love the thrill of the chase.

GNs will exaggerate and brag about their wins. Their desire to be social is fueled by a constant motivation to promote their conquistador, larger-than-life image. They are notorious for using any resource possible, especially technology and digital media, for self-promotion (e.g., see the history of Trump and Twitter). Jordan's gregarious nature is blatant if you saw *The Wolf of Wall Street*, in which he relentlessly brags about how much money he made, how many drugs he could pump into his body, and how many women he could have sex with on any given day. Gregariousness is having a Hollywood movie about how you swindled millions from innocent people, ended up in jail, and still came out on top.

Grandiose narcissists devalue tenderness, empathy, and loyalty. They repeatedly betray their lovers' trust, leaving their partners confused and wounded. Empathy is the ability to understand a lover's needs, perspectives, and feelings. An empathetic person feels guilt and remorse when hurting a lover and apologizes. In contrast, a GN will often say he and his lover had a "tiff" or a "small argument" after violently losing his temper, causing his lover severe emotional pain.

Maybe your PL cheated on you, leaving you crushed by betrayal. When confronted, he says, "Really? This again? It was only massages at a parlor." His denial and minimization of your pain twist the knife that's already in your heart. A PL's minimization of your suffering is more painful than the pain his original betrayal or abuse caused.

GNs are also ruthlessly self-centered. They are motivated by their selfish needs for pleasure and profit, which they will put above everything else, and their happiness is tied to the amount of sexual and financial gratification they can attain. GNs believe they are above the law. Noncompliance is highly connected to antisocial behavior. We've seen this play out in businesspeople like Bernie Madoff, Donald Trump, and Jeffrey Epstein.

Vulnerable (Covert) Narcissism

A person with low self-esteem who is depressed, anxious, selfish, and hostile may be classified as a vulnerable or covert narcissist (VN). Like their grandiose counterpart, VNs interact with others in a hostile, disagreeable manner (antagonistic). Yet what separates the VN from the GN is their high neuroticism. They are often called "thin-skinned narcissists." They are often harder to spot, as they are not as flamboyant and social as the grandiose narcissist.

VNs have low trust and are, therefore, highly suspicious and para-noid of others.[8] The VN believes that others are out to get him. A distrustful lover controls whom their partner spends time with.

In addition, if VNs feel inadequate, instead of reflecting on their pain and letting their partner know they are struggling, they will resort to temper tantrums over anything and everything and will always point fingers and blame. They will also lie to their partners' faces to meet their pleasure needs, such as when Larry told Juno he was going to work, but she caught him walking out of a hotel with his lover.

Like their grandiose counterparts, VNs are also prone to infidelity, gaslighting behaviors, and minimization of their partner's pain. VNs tend to be much more anxious and depressed than their grandiose coun-terparts, making them more insecure. Their personality is fragile.

The VN likely has a mood disorder (such as generalized anxi-ety disorder, some variety of depressive disorder, or bipolar disorder). Their mood disorders result in a diminished sense of agency com-pared to their grandiose counterpart. Hence, they are not as successful as their partners and parasitically live off them, either financially or emotionally, by associating with partners who boost their image.

VNs are antagonistic pessimists, meaning they are cynical and sus-picious partners.[9] They often misread their lovers' actions as attempts to harm them intentionally. And due to their high anger and hostility, they explode and punish. When Larry demanded that Juno quit her job and she pushed back, Larry gave her the silent treatment until she finally left. The VN's paranoid beliefs justify their need to be abusive to make their lover submissive.

VNs are highly vulnerable and come across as very needy and unable to handle stress. No amount of love or reassurance will fill the great emptiness of a VN. Their need for contact is insatiable. Due to their high vulnerability, they blame their wives for not satisfying needs that can never be satisfied. When the VN fails or feels rejected, they become ashamed.

BORDERLINE PERSONALITY DISORDER

Men with BPD exhibit extreme emotional behaviors in their relationships, as they struggle with a great deal of psychic pain. PLs who have BPD traits are "stably unstable." They are initially confident but become clingy due to their haunting fear of abandonment and are more likely to react angrily in intimate relationships due to this deep fear. Their anger often drives their partners away. BPD men can behave in self-centered ways, like narcissists. They differ because they want to bond and share intimacy, yet due to their emotional reactivity, it can be challenging.

They can suffer from depression because of their intense internal stress. And such men often struggle with reflecting on their depression and getting to the root of it. Instead, they get angry, act jealous, and blame their partners when things go wrong in the relationship.

Loving a man with BPD traits can feel like living on an emotional roller coaster. They are hypersensitive and can perceive a harmless comment as a giant insult. Their lack of trust and emotional dysregulation fuels their coercive control. And they are often impulsive to calm their emotions. BPD is the most common disorder for which people seek therapy, and it is highly treatable.

Most people with a personality disorder have more than one.[10] Their excess of toxic traits is the pathological foundation of the trauma bond.

Psychopathy

The concept of psychopathy has a rich historical tradition. Sandra L. Brown, MA's research has demonstrated that the pathological lover in a TBR has psychopathic traits. Although the diagnosis is not in the *Diagnostic and Statistical Manual of Mental Disorders (DSM)*, it can be added as a specifier onto an ASPD diagnosis.[11] The term psychopathy was introduced into mainstream society by psychiatrist Hervey M. Cleckley in 1941 in his groundbreaking book *The Mask of Sanity*.[12]

Cleckley described the successful psychopath as a superficially charming and guiltless social predator who achieves personal success and avoids jail.

In 1985, forensic psychologist Robert Hare developed the Psychopathy Checklist (PCL).[13] He described a psychopath as a charismatic, grandiose, shallow freeloader who lies, manipulates, and lacks empathy.

At the cornerstone of the "affectionless psychopath" is their inability to form tender attachments with others. Unfortunately, this does not stop others from bonding with them. Psychopaths are criminals in their hearts and see connections through the lens of "prey-predator pursuits," which is how they rationalize dominating and lying to their lovers.[14] They are emotional zombies toward their lovers' feelings and can feel emotions only about themselves.[15] Hello, Dirty John!

A psychopath's love strategy is fast and furious; they seek immediate gratification and take what they want. Without a conscience, they regard sexual contact with absolute casualness and are serial cheaters. Dating apps are a psychopath's dream because the availability of casual sex on dating apps allows them to indulge in one-night stands.

Like narcissists, psychopaths may be grandiose; they happily belittle their lovers and feel entitled to act abusively because they feel superior.[16] Narcissists and psychopaths have also been associated with leadership positions; their traits are regarded as necessary and desirable qualities of a strong leader. Yikes! James Bond certainly has some of these qualities—his bold fearlessness makes him appealing and highly successful.[17]

Psychopathy and ASPD share traits.[18] And these traits aren't exclusive to murderers and serial killers; no, they are common in the everyday man. They are intermittently abusive, cold-hearted lovers who remain emotionally detached despite dramatic displays of affection. They are manipulative, pathological liars. Authentic intimacy with a psychopath is impossible because their promises don't match their actions. They manipulate others by making empty promises of change and have no problem exploiting others to meet their needs for money, pleasure, and power. Psychopaths are dominant and cocky.

For example, Nick displayed extreme aggression and violence when he threw his daughter into the car trunk. Jordan showed this side when he kicked me down the stairs and reversed our car into the garage door while I was hanging halfway out of it. Psychopaths can abuse and control their lovers because they view people as objects to use, not partners to love.

They lack empathy, remorse, and compassion, making them mean and insensitive. Psychopaths are also irresponsible, unambitious, impulsive, and unethical. This combination makes them behave like a lazy teenager looking for instant gratification. They lack self-discipline and don't have a conscience.[19] So, they can never follow through on their promises. They take forever getting around to doing what you ask of them (if they do it all). Psychopaths also deny personal responsibility for their role in conflict of any kind or the way their life is going.

And just like a child, the psychopath is impulsive, so they don't think before acting and are driven by a need to feel pleasure. When you combine the two traits, you get someone who is hasty, gives in to every desire, and blames others when caught. We saw this play out between Larry and Juno when she confronted him about having an affair. Recall that Larry threatened suicide initially and then later made Juno believe everything was her fault, saying they were in a "dead marriage before the affair." He later threatened to cheat on her if she didn't lose weight, even though he had already started sleeping with someone else by that point.

A psychopath is also someone who can intentionally harm their lover and not feel remorse. They have a diminished capacity for experiencing a wide range of emotions and an inability to understand the emotions and feelings of others. Their emotional shallowness allows them to be ruthless and exploit their partners' trust. They lack a conscience and are incapable of feeling remorse. And since they view other people as mere pawns in their game, they lack empathy.

What they lack in *feeling*, they make up for with high *action*. Psychopathic, bold fearlessness allows PLs to take financial risks or gamble with other people's money. They disregard moral and ethical standards upon being presented with an opportunity to benefit themselves. Many pathological lovers will break the law to gain wealth and success.

For example, emotionless executives can exploit their employees, and con artists trick elderly pensioners. Their emotional detachment allows them to see people as utility belts to meet their insatiable need for power, status, and pleasure.

Like the grandiose narcissist, psychopaths seek high excitement through substance use and scenarios that create an adrenaline rush. Recall Jason's lifestyle of using drugs and engaging in every dangerous sexual scheme imaginable, Larry's alcohol use and extramarital affairs, and Nick's secret double life as a bisexual man.

Like the grandiose narcissist, psychopaths are superficially charming and bold. Their charm is alluring, but it wears off like Cinderella's dress at midnight. After the charm is gone, you're left with the psychopath's high assertiveness, a trait that makes them fearless, intimidating, and threatening. Nick threatened Keri with physical and verbal violence, claiming she would leave their marriage only through death. Larry dominated Juno by manipulating the police, flipping the script, and obtaining a restraining order against her. Tom intimidated Alex with belligerent, defensive, and contemptuous verbal abuse. High assertiveness is a foundational trait for pathological lovers' control.

THE DARK TETRAD

Since 2002, personality researchers have classified **narcissistic, psychopathic, Machiavellian**, and **sadistic** personality categories under the umbrella term Dark Tetrad (DT). While each has distinct antiso-cial traits, all four types share low remorse and hostile antagonism.[20] The DT describes those with subclinical features of the above catego-ries, meaning that individuals possess high levels of the characteristics. Still, they do not reach the level to classify them as a personality disor-der. Regardless, DT individuals destroy their lovers and leave disaster in their wake.

DT individuals have the same amoral values and beliefs as patho-logical lovers. People are tools to manipulate and use, and the DT's mantra of "great things should come to me, and if they don't, I'll make them" justifies their pathological selfishness. Thus far, we have covered that a pathological lover has narcissistic and psychopathic personality traits; let's add two more from the Dark Tetrad traits: Machiavellianism and sadism.

Machiavellianism

Machiavellian is derived from Niccolo Machiavelli, a sixteenth-century Florentine politician known for his deceptive, cruel, and corrupt politi-cal ideas. Machiavellian individuals are master manipulators and have a game-playing attitude when in love. They will text another lover to meet up for sex while lying in bed next to you, and they rotate among three women simultaneously to relieve stress and fulfill their need for sexual variety.[21]

Machiavellian men have a unique capacity to assess their lov-ers' thoughts and use this information for manipulative purposes. One patient who grew up in the Midwest with a cruel mother and cold father told me that when she first met her husband, he told her, "I always wanted to meet a sweet young girl from the Midwest that I could save."

Machiavellian individuals use softer tactics to influence others and are good at faking love. They make excellent salesmen since they can lie through their teeth. When they first meet you, they will look into your eyes and adamantly profess their love and commitment to you: "You make me so happy; I never want to lose you." They will compare themselves to their equally degenerate friends, saying, "All my friends stay out late, and I used to do that too, but now I love coming home early to be with you." However, a year and a half into the TBR, you will discover they have lived a secret double life of wild infidelity from the start—while traveling "for work," going to "see family." The character Stephen DeMarco in the drama *Tell Me Lies* is an excellent example of a Machiavellian lover.[22] In the show, you see him masterfully have two serious relationships simultaneously at the same college without either woman knowing for a long time.

And just like Machiavelli, they do not act alone. Some of their close friends, roommates, or business associates are entangled in the Machiavellian's elaborate web of lies. They are the gatekeepers to his impenetrable wall of secrecy—and they're just as sweet, charming, and deceitful as him.

Psychopaths and Machiavellians are experts at concealing their true nature and intentionally hiding displeasing personal information. Thus, they can initially wear a "healthy mask" that covers their inner swindler. Their partners are nothing more than convenient stepping stones for their gratification of sex, social status, and financial gain.

Sadism

In the late nineteenth century, Richard von Krafft-Ebing first introduced the term "sadism" in his foundational work, *Psychopathia Sexualis*, defining it as deriving pleasure from another's pain and suffering.[23] A sadistic lover experiences pleasure through inflicting or witnessing another's physical or emotional pain. Sadists feel joy when observing the suffering of people they know, especially their lovers.

A sadist longing to see others' humiliation motivates them to dominate and control their partners. They derive pleasure from intentionally instilling fear in others or saying cruel things to their partners, such as, "That's why you're still single at forty-four. Nobody wants your sorry old ass."

Sexual sadism is the wish to control another person by inflicting pain. For sadists, physically harming their lover during sex produces sexual arousal and pleasure; lust and cruelty are intertwined. Sadistic lovers abuse their lovers without their consent. They often brand their lovers with their initials by cutting them into their skin. Rapists and sexual predators are sadists.

An excellent modern-day example of this is Armie Hammer. Armie Hammer's alleged texts to his lovers exhibit a wide range of sadism related to cannibalism, bondage, and violence. Armie's behavior is sadistic and is not BDSM. In BDSM, two consenting and well-informed partners agree to engage in sexual role play, which results in a safe and sexually gratifying experience.

Sadistic men are unlikely to lend a sympathetic ear. Instead, they tend to be more critical or sarcastic when you need empathy. This willingness to criticize you applies to your successes, too. While others may cheer you on after your victory, sadistic PLs will mock, insult, or ignore you—they cannot tolerate being out of the limelight.

One of my patients has a three-year restraining order against her ex-husband because he abused her and their children, whom he lost custody of in the divorce. While they were married, he would force her to have sex, and then the moment he was finished, he would immediately cast her aside and say things such as, "That was the worst sex I have ever had. I just wanted a piece of ass." He derived pleasure from being cruel to her after using her. Sadists love to witness their partners' (or ex-partners') pain when wounding them.

A famous sadist is the mythical Don Juan, who seduced and abandoned women, going to great lengths to humiliate them publicly: "Even more than seduction, the greatest pleasure is to trick women and leave them dishonored."[24] Enjoying cruelty and inflicting harm are

Dark Tetrad & ASPD Trait Overlap

APSD TRAITS	NARCISSISM	PSYCHOPATHY	MACHIAVELLIAN	SADISM
MANIPULATIVE	✓	✓	✓	
CALLOUS	✓	✓	✓	✓
DECEITFUL	✓	✓	✓	
HOSTILE	✓	✓	✓	✓
RISK TAKING	✓	✓	✓	
IMPULSIVE	✓	✓		✓
IRRESPONSIBLE	✓	✓		

Credit: Daniel J. Fox, *Antisocial, Narcissistic, and Borderline Personality Disorders: A New Conceptualization of Development, Reinforcement, Expression, and Treatment* (Routledge, 2020).

unique characteristics of sadism. A propensity for hurting others for sadistic pleasure is not limited to sadism and psychopathy; it is also part of narcissism's negative side.

ADDICTIONS, COMPULSIONS, IMPULSIVITY, AND MOOD DISORDERS

Pathological lovers usually have one or two substance addictions (drugs or alcohol), which makes it difficult to determine whether the toxic behavior is substance-induced or their true personality. They are likely to be dependent on illegal drugs or pharmaceutical addictive drugs.[25] This adds to the victim's hope and psychological confusion. Is he an addict or an abuser? Substance addiction causes physical dependence; when the drug or drink is out of the blood, there is a craving to replenish it. Substance abuse cannot *turn* a man into an abuser; it brings out what's already there and can make a PL more dangerous.

PLs who struggle with insomnia, depression, jealousy, and anxiety numb out these experiences with drugs, alcohol, or rage to override the painful feelings they cannot tolerate.

Compulsivity

In addition to a personality disorder and substance addiction, pathological lovers can also have compulsivity disorders. Compulsions are intrusive actions that must be carried out or addictions to a process. They manifest as uncontrollable and excessive sexuality (porn viewing, masturbating, paying for sex), gambling, or spending. PLs tend to compulsively act out sexually through a series of affairs or other casual sexual behaviors. Compulsive sexuality makes it possible to see other sexual partners for years without bonding with them. This is also a powerful strategy since it reduces the risk of rejection and abandonment, providing sexual jugglers with a reassuring safety net of sexual alternatives.

Impulsivity

Whereas compulsive behavior is premeditated, impulsive behavior is action without thought. Unless they have strong Machiavellian tendencies, PLs are also impulsive; they act without thinking and cannot control their behavior.[26] You feel their lack of self-control through their brash expressions of rage. One of the PL's favorite manipulation tools is to react with supreme anger to an innocent insult. They will punish you severely for even the most minor offense. You could make an off-hand comment they will take as a direct insult. Also, impulsivity is why PLs engage in reckless risk-taking, such as chronic acts of infidelity.[27]

Mood Disorders

Mood disorders, such as major depressive disorder, generalized anxiety disorder, and bipolar disorder, are common in PLs. Bipolar disorder is a mixture of severe depression and manic mood. One of my patients married a man who knew he had bipolar disorder and never told her. She only found out five years later by Googling the prescription she discovered in his medicine cabinet. A PL who has anxiety or depression and doesn't know it or acknowledge it means they don't treat it. And then their undiagnosed and untreated mood disorders are another match to light the fuel of their control and cruelty.

A pathological lover's personality has many layers: they can have overlapping pathological traits or personality disorders (narcissism, psychopathy, Machiavellianism, sadism), a mood disorder (depression, anxiety, bipolar), and a mixture of addictions and compulsions sprinkled in. Teasing apart these four complex layers is daunting, even for a well-trained therapist and personality expert. I hope you are experiencing self-compassion for having survived an impossibly difficult pathological personality and for having the courage to learn about who they are.

PLs' antisocial values and cruel behaviors traumatize their lovers. Their personality layers create a two-faced persona like Dr. Jekyll (a good, unaggressive, and charming self) and Mr. Hyde (a mean, aggressive, controlling, and abusive self). The two parts of the PL leave their partner with the confusing task of reconciling them. The financial, physical, psychological, and emotional wreckage they cause is profoundly debilitating. Yet, education can help you recover from the aftermath of loving a PL and allow your emotional self to become wiser about love and relationships.

I hope you now have a general awareness of the pathological lover's personality. I am confident you also have more self-compassion for yourself and the impossible personality you were (or are) up against. This should help explain why even the smartest women can get sucked into a PL's web.

By recognizing the complexity of a pathological lover's personality, you can understand why it feels so confusing to be in love with them. Let's move on to the next chapter, on trauma bonding, where I will explain the pathological lover's tactics and typical trauma bond phases.

PATHOLOGICAL LOVER CHECKLIST

How much of your partner do you see in the following behaviors?

- Speaks disrespectfully about his former partners
- Is deceitful; you catch him in lies
- Is disrespectful toward, belittles, and insults you
- Is dominating, wants to control your behavior, and restricts whom you connect with
- Blames you for everything
- Is possessive and unnecessarily jealous
- Lacks remorse, guilt, or compassion
- Is intimidating and threatening, expressing intense rage
- Is manipulative and gaslights you
- Is superficially charming in public
- Has double standards
- Shows sexual promiscuity
- Exhibits impulsivity and reckless driving, spending, or sex
- Fails to take accountability for the harm he causes you
- Has a grandiose personality and exaggerates his achievements and talents
- Abuses drugs and alcohol
- Requires excessive admiration and appreciation
- Considers himself superior and special

- Feels entitled to unreasonable expectations or automatic compliance with his expectations
- Is regularly aggressive in his communication
- Has the opposite emotional response to what is appropriate for the situation
- Does not respect boundaries
- Exploits others to make money or get ahead
- Has a parasitic lifestyle, living off others
- Has extreme mood changes
- Says words that don't match his actions
- Is superficial, with a shallow emotional expression

KEY POINTS TO REMEMBER

1. A **pathological lover** can have a mixture of Cluster B personality traits, a mood disorder, addictions, compulsions, and impulsions.

   a. **Cluster B personality disorders**: narcissistic personality disorder (grandiose or vulnerable), borderline personality disorder, and antisocial personality disorder.

   b. **Mood disorders**: generalized anxiety disorder, any variation of depressive disorder, and bipolar disorder.

   c. **Addictions, compulsions, and impulsivity**: Pathological lovers usually have one or two substance addictions, are compulsive cheaters, and are emotionally impulsive (usually rage and sex).

2. The **five-factor model of personality** (FFM, also known as the Big Five) is a highly regarded and scientifically valid measure of personality. It captures five categories of universal personality traits: **openness, conscientiousness, extraversion, agreeableness,** and **neuroticism.**

3. The **Dark Tetrad** is a term used to describe antisocial personality traits that don't quite meet the level that make them personality disorders. The Dark Tetrad includes **narcissism, psychopathology, Machiavellianism, and sadism.**

3 | Trauma Bonding

Relationships of inevitable harm occur when we have a level of
expectation that is not equal to our partner's level of disorder.[1]

—DR. SANDRA L. BROWN, MA

NOW THAT YOU KNOW WHAT a pathological lover's personality looks like and how they act, let's dive into how trauma bonding with one occurs. After all, if they're so awful, how do so many intelligent and kind women get sucked into relationships with them? What initial tactics does the PL use to create such a compelling emotional attachment? What behaviors does he apply to control and manipulate? In other words, if you've ever wondered, "I'm a smart woman, how could this have happened to me?" this chapter answers that question. We take a deep dive into the PL's insincere love tactics, psychological manipulation, and typical phases of traumatic bonding. Remember that darker behaviors of love, such as coercion and psychological violence, occur because the pathological lover engages you in a cycle of intermittent harm and care. He creates and then exploits a power imbalance due to feeling entitled and having self-centered values.

Recall that traumatic bonding occurs from two conditions: intermittent abuse and a power difference. Power is the ability to influence another person's behaviors, and control is the main goal for a PL. Experiencing insensitivity and betrayal by people you initially trusted and believed becomes highly traumatizing and leaves you feeling helpless and confused.

The harmful dynamics in TBRs are also referred to as intimate partner violence (IPV).[2] Violence is defined as the intentional harm of another person. In TBRs, the pathological lover feels entitled to have more power over their lover and assert their authority through hurtful behaviors of domination and manipulation. And PLs use calculated deception to meet their needs for pleasure, which confuses their partners.

Of course, the love connection does not start abusively; it initially feels exciting and passionate. There is electricity—maybe in a way you have never felt before. Your lover's kindness and obsessive attention create an ambiance of trust.

Yet over time, your PL has moments of mistreating you. You see signs of deception ("I never said that I wasn't still on dating apps. You just assumed that without asking."), manipulation ("Oh, my ex was such a narcissist. It's great to meet a compassionate woman finally."), or dominance ("If you don't quit your job for me, you don't love me."). Or maybe he says he does not want to be exclusive yet becomes enraged when you date or sleep with someone else.

Additionally, PLs are furious and highly defensive when you question them; they morph into a person you can hardly recognize. This leaves you confused because just a few days ago, they'd said, "I love spending time with you. I haven't felt love in such a long time. I'm so glad we found each other." So, you sit around hurt and waiting for them to cool off, thinking of ways you can help repair the connection. Then, Romeo comes to his senses, saying he is sorry for reacting like that and will never do it again. (Intermittent abuse.) You sigh in relief and get off the emotional roller coaster you've just been riding. You offer up the solutions you've strategized in your mind, and he agrees to them, creating a sense of hope that all will be well moving forward. The love potion of intense passion and savvy manipulation puts you in a trance, making you immune to his harmful behavior.

Does any of this sound familiar?

I compare this naivete about PLs to the myth of "invisible ships." This phenomenon was supposedly described by researchers who studied Christopher Columbus's arrival on the coast of what would become the West Indies. The folklore proposes that the indigenous people could not see such enormous ships in plain sight approaching the shore. They had no mental representations of such vessels because they had never seen one before. So, when danger approached, they couldn't see it coming. This chapter will explain the typical phases of a trauma bond so you will not miss a PL's underhanded tactics. You will see the danger on the horizon. No more invisible ships!

THE PHASES OF TRAUMA BONDING

The Sweet Seduction Phase:
Hunting and Love-Conning

Even pathological people want love. However, they don't wear signs saying, "I am looking for a lover to betray and abuse who will meet all my needs for power and pleasure." No, PLs do the opposite—they seek vulnerable targets and lure them in by presenting themselves as charming, strong, honest, and dependable.[3] No wonder it's so easy to fall for them. Thoroughly captivated by your every word, they are likable. You think to yourself, "Wow, this guy truly hears me." Traumatic bonds begin with promises of love, trust, and tenderness because the PL's early behavior implies the two of you will meet each other's emotional needs.

However, those with self-centered beliefs and personality patholo-gies like narcissistic personality disorder (NPD), antisocial personality disorder (ASPD), and psychopathy are more likely to envision relation-ships like predatory wolves. Their behavior is driven by their mercenary motivation to seek out unassuming targets, which can be used to feed them. PLs hunt for the scent of opportunity and vulnerability.

Whenever you experience the end of a relationship, losing a par-ent, or being fired, you experience the pain of life's inevitable cruelties. The PL will exploit your suffering and prey on your losses by faking empathy to create an emotional bond. New beginnings and significant life changes, such as moving to a new city or starting university, can also make us feel insecure and vulnerable. The PL will try to become everything you have lost, are longing for, or are missing. Lily's obsessive desire to become valedictorian due to her low self-esteem drove her to cut herself off from letting loose and having fun. So, when fun-loving, exciting, attention-doting Jason came into the picture, she was hooked.

PLs concentrate on our delicately programmed human need for love. Humans are social beings and thrive when they feel they mat-ter. To feel appreciated is a normal human desire. Like Juno, who felt excited by her love's ability to heal Larry's gambling addiction, we all want to be valued for our potential and ability to make a difference in our lovers' lives. A PL will acknowledge your usefulness.

The PL chooses and affirms a competent woman because he is look-ing for someone who can boost his image for his gain or whom he can parasitically live off to use for his self-interest. If you've ever wondered why and how such smart women can end up with these pathological men—this is one of the reasons. PLs specifically seek them out.

Victims are targeted and seduced precisely because the perpetra-tor counts on them being blind to his true intentions. Your PL is confident and bold, just like Armie Hammer. "Con man" is a short-ened version of "confidence man." Whenever you meet someone new, you present the best of yourself. In Jungian psychology, this is called

your persona.[4] The word "persona" was used in Roman times to sig-
nify a mask worn by an actor. The persona represents the social mask
we each "wear" to portray our personality to others. Yet a PL deceiv-
ingly manufactures a whole persona and intentionally misrepresents
himself to entice his target into a relationship. He fakes a persona
of confidence, charm, security, and interest and performs the love-
conning behaviors of rescuing you from your pain. And you have no
clue that his premeditated behavior is love-conning. You soak in his
kindness like a thirsty flower.

LOVE-BOMBING

Smooth operators give you excessive affection, attention, and flattery
and lavish you with trips, gifts, and promises during the love-bombing
phase.[5] It can be a thoughtful card, message, or a watch, any of which
implies that you are in the PL's heart and mind. The attention and
contact come from constant texting, sexting, calling, or dropping by,
suggesting he is obsessed with being connected to you. He finds out
you are sick; he sends chicken soup to you at work. He constantly tells
you you're stunning; you're the beauty to his beast, and he can't believe
he has a woman like you.

Love-bombing draws you in like a magnet, makes you feel incredible, and works as a potent distraction that disables you from seeing
behind your PL's mask. As you revel in the attention, affection, and
excitement of finding the perfect partner, you start believing you can
trust this guy and slowly grow to depend on him for love and security.

Tom's love-bombing gave a new meaning to Alex's being "swept
off her feet." Their desire was magnetic; they could not stay away from
each other. Tom's seductive tactics fit Alex's deep desire to matter to
someone. Alex explained, "It felt so good to be intensely pursued and
desired all the time. I felt honored that a man of his caliber would find
me captivating, beautiful, and intelligent."

INTENSITY

Pathological lovers date at warp speed to keep you off-balance before recognizing their antisocial nature. They push for phone calls, regular dates, short trips away, have you meet all their friends and family, and ask or demand commitment at the climax of their seduction when it feels impossible and irrational to say no. This intense timing goes together with the love-bombing phase. Your partner seduces you to earn your trust, so you overlook any emerging red flags or inconsistencies in his persona. His unrelenting pursuit and fast and furious passion feel emotionally overwhelming. It can be hard to think and act rationally when flooded with emotions.

Jason pursued Lily relentlessly in the beginning. She described how they went on a date nearly every night within the first three weeks of their relationship. He texted her throughout the day, planned fun things for them to do, nights would end with passionate sex, and mornings would pick up right where they left off. He was communicative and emotionally open. One month in, he asked her to be exclusive while the two were high on Molly; she recalls waking up feeling confused, trapped, yet excited. Just as he began phasing out the intensity of their first month together, he started initiating plans for several weeks or months ahead, creating emotional and psychological confusion for Lily. But it was too late; she was already hooked. Only one month in, she couldn't bring herself to leave. This is how potent, dangerous, and effective a PL's calculated tactics are.

TWINSHIP

Alex was deeply in love with Tom, and his love-bombing fooled her into thinking she could be physically and emotionally safe with him. She blindly let Tom into her heart and told him everything she loved— Italian food, tennis, historical novels—and was shocked to find that he loved the same things! She thought she'd found herself a unicorn.

Alex now understands Tom was faking his enjoyment of the same food, books, and activities she liked. Tom's deceit about personal taste is called twinship. This is when the PL purposely mirrors his partner's likes and dislikes to imply that they are perfectly compatible.[6] He claims to have the same life experiences, which becomes a point of mutual bonding. The target feels significant, and her trust deepens.

We also saw this in the dynamic between Jason and Lily, with Jason talking about how thankful he was for therapy upon finding out that Lily was pursuing a career as a therapist. The PL will often let you do all the talking in the beginning, or he will constantly ask questions about you, your experiences, and your preferences to gather as much information before the mic gets passed on to him. While having someone hang on every word you say might feel deeply affirming, it can be a red flag you don't want to miss.

Many women confuse the intensity of their romance with love, the twinship with being soulmates, and the passion with authentic bonding—all painful oversights. As you can see, trauma bonding happens quickly and subtly and is disguised as uncontrollable desire. The relationship's fast-paced development is thrilling and hypnotic, but the intensity is not intimacy.

Read that again.

Because of the ongoing manipulative love tactics, your nervous system becomes ungrounded. Love-bombing is so extreme that it creates a flood of the feel-good neurotransmitter dopamine in the brain. This is the same neurotransmitter that makes it hard to stop reaching for another late-night cookie and drives the addictive cycle of cocaine use.

Oxytocin is a bonding hormone released when you experience physical intimacy, orgasm, and affection with another person. Because love-bombing happens so intensely and quickly, your body becomes flooded with dopamine and oxytocin, creating a physical addiction to the chemicals and reinforcing your dependency and bond. "Love" literally becomes a drug.

MIND MAPPING

Initially, the PL allows the target to do all the talking while he listens intently to learn about her lifelong goals. The social predator is mind mapping the target to understand what makes her life meaningful, what type of people she is drawn to, and what she values. He asks all the right questions and makes her feel heard, validated, and supported.

Mind mapping comes from the psychological principle "theory of mind," which refers to the realization we experience in early development that others possess beliefs and desires different from our own.[7] We can predict other people's behaviors and anticipate their responses by understanding what's in their minds. So once the PL gathers information about your psychological makeup, he applies it to manipulate you into falling for him.

Many pop culture resources, therapists, and theories have pushed the narrative that pathological lovers are deficient in empathy. Empathy is the human capacity to understand how another person's experiences emotionally affect them. Empathy is multidimensional. *Cognitive* (thinking) *empathy* is the ability to know what another person feels. This is the most well-known form of empathy and what we often engage in when we attempt to put ourselves in someone else's shoes. In comparison, *emotional empathy* is being able to peer inside another person and feel what they are feeling and, if appropriate, feel compassion toward them. Emotional empathy is fundamental for social bonding and cooperation.

Contrary to popular belief, PLs are not entirely devoid of empathy. The couple's therapist David Schnarch writes that pathological lovers have *antisocial empathy*.[8] Empathy is not always linked to prosocial (positive) motivations, such as a person wanting to resonate with your pain. The PL pays attention to your every word and breath not because he is genuinely interested in you but because he must understand you to control you. Both manipulation and deception require recognizing and understanding their target's thoughts, desires, and emotions. PLs use mind mapping and apply antisocial empathy to find their lovers' weak spots to manipulate them.

Mind mapping is a tactic that the PL uses initially to gather information on his target. Yet he utilizes this information to dominate and manipulate his lover more in the middle phase of the relationship. For example, Tom knew Alex's dad left home when Alex was young and never returned, so Alex deeply feared abandonment. After a night of Tom insulting Alex, calling her a lazy, stupid whore, she screamed at him, "Tom, the only reason anyone puts up with you is for the perks, for the money!" That statement must have struck a chord in Tom because he said he was leaving.

"See all of this?" he yelled. "The house, your life, five-star vacations . . . this is all gone without me!" Following Alex's father's footsteps, he left the house despite Alex clinging to him, begging him not to go, and saying she was so sorry. Terrified, Alex stayed awake all night. Yet Tom never called and did not come home.

When Tom did return late the next afternoon, Alex was so relieved that she apologized and swore she would never lash out at him again. Tom smiled, petted her head, and said, "Good girl, now go and pack for that vacation we planned for this week."

This vignette shows examples of antisocial empathy; Tom ripped open Alex's core wound of abandonment and used it to knock her into submission. Threats followed by hope are a prime example of the pattern of intermittent reinforcement. Alex's behavior was controlled and changed through processes of punishment and reward. Tom taught her that if she fought back, she would suffer; Alex learned it was not worth it.

PLs can also be *dark empaths*.[9] Dark empaths don't only lack empathy; they have the opposite emotional response to what is appropriate to the situation. Therefore, empathy deficits entail the presence of inappropriate emotions. For example, when Juno explained to Larry the pain she felt due to his betrayal, instead of resonating with her hurt, he ignored her suffering and attacked her even more. Dark empaths who are exceptionally high in the sadism trait enjoy hurting their partner or gain pleasure from witnessing their partner's suffering. The Germans have a word for this, *schadenfreude*. It is a compound of *schaden,* meaning "damage" or "harm," and *freude* meaning "joy," which translates to finding joy in someone else's pain.[10] The dark empath lives by schadenfreude; he relishes his lover's despair.

A PL also strategically monopolizes your time and focus so he can continually implant images into your mind. He does this directly by spending time with you, texting, or calling, and indirectly by suggesting you watch his favorite movies, sending you a playlist of his favorite songs, or telling you what his favorite book is so you read it (and if he's good, they'll all have romantic undertones). He's priming you to do and feel what *he* wants.

Romantic language activates your emotions and creates pictures in your mind.[11] Expressions such as "we are two peas in a pod," "love at first sight," "you stole my heart," and "eternal flame" elicit eternal bond images in your mind. Superior mind mapping from the PL also creates the illusion of validation because you feel someone identifies with you. PLs use their antisocial empathy skills to affirm your feelings and initially meet your needs.

Middle Phase: The Trauma Vortex

The middle phase of a trauma bond begins when the PL reveals characteristics that conflict with how he initially presented himself. As the relationship develops, the woman loses a sense of personal control and power in both her life and the relationship. During this phase, the PL becomes meaner, more dominant, and more emotionally manipulative, causing her to feel confused and immobilized. And the woman feels absolute pressure to comply with the PL's demands to avoid conflict and loss of affection.

At this point in the relationship, you suddenly feel like you are drowning in your emotions. One minute feels fine—then *bang!*—you're emotionally decimated. Your feelings of self-worth begin to evaporate. You're alive and look mildly functional to the world, but the world doesn't see your paralysis and confusion. You feel like you'll be stuck in this anxious-depressed state forever without any hope of change.

This is what I call the *trauma vortex*. A vortex is a feeling or situation with so much influence over you that you feel you are not in control. You're no longer in la-la land with your unicorn; you're walking through an emotional battlefield where there are hidden psychological landmines everywhere. Let's unpack each one.

COERCIVE CONTROL AND DOMINATION

A PL uses psychological bullying and aggressive domination to establish power and total control over you.[12] The first is *authority*. Big and small decisions are made in intimate relationships, but the PL wants to be the boss, and he'll find any way to do it. Like a bloodthirsty beast, the more control he gets, the more he wants. For example, Tom would say to Alex, "Do what I tell you" and "We will go out when I say we go out." Initially, Alex would argue back, but Tom verbally whiplashed her with his rage. Alex learned to submit to his demands to de-escalate his anger; his happiness mattered to her.

Jason, who initially introduced Lily to partying with drugs, would never ensure her responsible use. On many occasions, he either gave her too much or let her blackout by mixing them with alcohol, and then he would berate her the following day. "You stupid bitch! You made a fool of me last night with how you behaved!" he would say. He'd make up elaborate stories about things she'd done and turn her blackouts against her, stating that she could not join him and his friends during nights out anymore.

If you have ever been viciously threatened, you understand immobilizing fear and submission. PLs enjoy aggressively dominating because it causes submission and creates self-doubt, making you easier to control. Also, forcing you to be subservient feeds a PL's grandiose ego. Then you lie to yourself, creating a convincing narrative that you believe: "He's only pressuring me so we can be on the same page because he loves me" or "He's just trying to have my back. Despite the things he says, he means well."

PLs use social alienation to solidify their power over you. He doesn't only keep a tight rein on your activities but also with whom you do things. If you try to set boundaries when he restricts your social circle, you're met with his aggressive threats and domination. Abusers will block you from seeing the people who matter most to you: your friends, family, and anyone watching out for your best interests. And they don't always do it directly, such as telling you that you are forbidden from seeing such and such. No, they start infiltrating your opinions of your friends, pointing out all the negatives in your loved ones, and drawing attention to issues in your relationships with them. Their psychological manipulation leads you to distance yourself from those you care about the most. Alienation also includes not telling people about the coercive control you are experiencing; you feel emotionally alone.

Or, once the PL has you wrapped around their finger, they can become unlikable to others. You think, "If only they could see all the good things in him that I see." You make more effort to bring him and your loved ones together, but your friends and family won't have it. They make the difficult decision to distance themselves from you, and since you're so enamored, you allow for the distance, thinking you're fine as long as you have him.

Whenever Keri and Nick went out with friends, Nick would be drunk and obnoxious toward everyone by the night's end. Naturally, their friends stopped wanting to hang out with them. Keri stated that she isolated herself from her friends and family because she was embarrassed by how Nick treated her and was ashamed of what she tolerated. Alex explained that many of her girlfriends stopped checking in with her because they were sick of her complaints about Tom's abuse and drama and tired of giving advice that she would never take.

A PL constantly monitors his partner's whereabouts with computers, electronic communications, and phone calls. A sadist loves to use surveillance, so he might search your phone, purse, pockets, car, and house to keep track of your time and money. Your dismay at having to tolerate this gives him pleasure. He might force you to check in regularly or demand you share your location from your phone so he can always verify where you are.

To this day, Lily, who is more technologically savvy than anyone, is still puzzled by how Jason manipulated her following one of their blowup fights. She had already caught him sexting other women, and their relationship lacked trust. Jason coerced her into sharing her location with him by offering to share his location with her—something she was convinced he would never, ever offer up. She breathed a sigh of relief and thought, "This is perfect. I have nothing to hide and everything to gain from being able to track him anytime, day or night. He wants to go out with the boys. I'll know exactly where he is. This will help me trust him now." A year later, she discovered he had been paying for sex with hookers on certain nights and had brought his phone. Meanwhile, his location always showed he was home. How was that even possible?

Intimate terrorists may also claim to protect you from others. One of my patients explained how her husband said to her parents, "I've had enough of you hurting Melinda. If you wanna speak to her, you gotta go through me now."

Controlling men will often call their wives or girlfriends multiple times throughout the day and expect an immediate response. Alex explained how Tom began exhibiting controlling behavior. "He wanted me to quit my job and every activity that took time away from being with him. He even got me a phone for only his calls, so I better answer when he calls or texts." Alex said she felt captive. Tom used electronic devices for surveillance to ensure she could not go to certain places or visit friends he disapproved of.

Setting boundaries will usually cause your PL to have hostile outbursts because they are proactively aggressive. Proactive aggression is organized, cold-blooded, and motivated by the anticipation of getting and demanding what you want.[13] Having healthy boundaries is normal and does not warrant threats and intimidation. Yet, you drop your boundaries to accommodate the PL again to salvage your well-being. The PL's domination continues to strip your confidence. By this point, you have unknowingly surrendered your power.

Complying with the PL's unnatural demands is an example of self-abandonment. When the PL plows through your boundaries and screams at you for expressing differing needs, you are bullied into disconnecting from your true desires. Abandoning your truth and needs creates another layer of insecurity that enables the PL to control you. You start to realize his love is transactional, while yours is unconditional. However, you feel dependent on his bread crumbs of care, so you rationalize your self-denial and sink deeper into despair.

BELITTLEMENT AND DISRESPECT

Belittlement and disrespect involve treating someone as inferior and not fully human. Constant criticism from the PL undermines your overall sense of well-being and self-worth.[14] Larry often said to Juno, "Do you think anyone else would want you? Look at all the weight you've gained since you broke your sobriety." Blindly in love initially, she passively shrugged off his insults. Jason would say to Lily, "Good luck finding someone else who will put up with your shit like I do. No one wants to deal with your baggage, and there's a lot of it. You're lucky I do." With her self-esteem already in the garbage, Lily would agree and thank him for loving her.

In public, your partner might celebrate you and boast to everyone about how beautiful and intelligent his wife is because he cares about his image. However, before you left the house, he probably criticized the dress you put on, said you're starting to age, and demanded you change because you look like a disgrace.

Alternatively, he could use psychological violence by calling you a bitch, whore, or other awful names. These insults assault your humanity, reducing you to an object. Depersonalizing you enables him to be free of remorse or guilt. And yes, a lack of remorse on the part of the PL contributes to his underlying insensitivity.

Your PL will always flip the script and claim to be the victim. The dictionary defines a victim as "one who suffers some hardship or loss and is badly treated or taken advantage of."[15] Being a victim can be a highly harmful experience resulting in psychological distress, fear, anxiety, and a diminished sense of power and trust. He cannot be the victim if he is the one who holds all the power. Based on what you have just read, does it sound like a PL is being victimized? So why does he claim he is your victim?

Psychological theories refer to this as *victim signaling*.[16] In this strategy, the PL portrays himself as a victim by complaining about all the distress and inconvenience your behavior has caused him. He is hypersensitive to any perceived slight, yet he constantly criticizes and blames you for everything. You don't appreciate him, you're cold, dismissive, or even a racist, and he must teach you how to be a better person so you don't harm others. PLs intentionally deploy this manipulative strategy to alter your behavior toward them. So, it is reasonable to assume that a self-promoting PL will lie about being a victim if they believe it is personally advantageous. The absence of a guiding moral compass—illustrated by their obsession with power, self-grandiosity, and general disregard for social norms—allows the PL to fake victimhood for personal gain without a single ounce of guilt.

Coercive control undermines your need for autonomy, which is psychological freedom, because you are forced to behave in ways that are not true to you. It also thwarts the need for genuine connection because it involves your PL withholding affection if you do not submit to his demands. Criticism makes you feel insecure and less competent in life. Your personal growth is halted due to your bond with a mentally unhealthy partner.

MIND GAMES AND MANIPULATION
Lying

Lying and omitting the truth strengthen a strategy of coercive control.[17] Deception makes a true partnership impossible but keeps the trauma bond going. PLs keep their partners confused or in the dark because they know we'll be long gone once we see them.

A PL can manipulate his partner by rationalizing his bad behavior. "I know I got home late last night. My colleague Andrew laid one on me during happy hour. He's been going through so much with his wife and needed to vent." You press him, and he refuses to answer questions, but he *aggressively* flips it back to you, "I was just being a good friend, and I get cross-examined by you? This is ridiculous." Or he offers illogical explanations such as, "I don't know what I was thinking, but I'd left my cell at the office and didn't realize until after we'd ordered drinks. I couldn't just leave." PLs can also produce an elaborate web of lies that are impossible to verify to cover up their double lives: "I guess Andrew and his wife had been trying for a while, and she finally conceived, but then she miscarried a few weeks ago, and she's been so depressed since then. They're not having sex, and it's affecting their relationship. Poor guy went on and on about how hard it's been." Of course, he does all of this to deflect the fact that he came home after midnight.

The PL's lies in the middle stage don't match the early love-bombing phase. One minute he is manipulating you with rage, and then he's wooing you back with pledges of love, gifts, and real change. The discrepancy in his actions causes you to question, "Is he a good guy or a monster? Do I love him or hate him?" The PL's rapid shift between the two sides of his personality creates an emotional change in you between love and hate, trust and distrust. You cannot hold one consistent view of him or your relationship: your lover's intentional confusion chains you to the TBR. Recall that intermittent abuse, which relates to his Dr. Jekyll/Mr. Hyde personality, creates an intense attachment.

No Remorse

From joy to sadness, humans have a wide range of emotions that enhance our experiences with others. Most of us have the necessary feelings of remorse, guilt, and compassion because we have a conscience, an inner feeling or voice guiding right from wrong. Conscience emotions help to curb our behaviors by stopping behaviors that cause our loved ones to suffer.

Yet, we cannot create emotionally safe relationships or resolve our fights with PLs because they lack remorse and compassion.[18] The PL's lack of accountability due to his lack of guilt is the knife in your heart. It's painful enough when someone cheats on you, lies to you, and abuses you, yet it becomes impossible to share intimacy with them when they deny or ignore the pain they have caused you.

Gaslighting

As the PL ups the ante, the gaslighting begins. Gaslighting is a method of psychological attack used to make you doubt your memory and perception of reality.[19] When you accuse a pathological lover of lying or cheating, they will not only lie and manipulate you but also blame you. By doing so, they deflect your attention because you are prone to self-reflect on how you contributed to the issue (as any healthy partner *would* do). PLs weaponize your conscience against you.

For example, Nick was the one always cheating on Keri. Yet whenever Keri wanted to go away with her girlfriends, he accused her of wanting to go on a trip just so that she could flirt with other men. Nick put Keri on the defense to direct her attention away from his philandering. Keri wondered if she'd ever done anything to give him the idea she would be with another man. When you question a PL about his betrayal, he makes it your fault; he makes you doubt your perception and manipulates you into believing his narrative is true. When Larry cheated on Juno, he blamed her, "I felt rejected by you, which made me cheat on you. I'm hurting too. I didn't want to, but you drove me to do it!" I even had one client whose husband took a picture of himself naked on top of another woman with the caption, "You made me do this."

Another word for gaslighting is *perspecticide*.[20] In the middle phase of the trauma vortex, your perspectives, desires, and opinions get wiped out due to your PL's domination. Or you may lose a sense that you even have the right to your viewpoint due to him controlling every aspect of your life. Perspecticide is the inability to connect to what you know. The PL erases your thoughts, feelings, voice, and perspective. Also, women feel erased when men objectify them. And the PL indeed objectifies his lover and uses her as a utility belt to fulfill his needs.

Lily recalls a moment toward the end of her relationship in which she was so gaslit that she felt genuinely crazy. She could no longer tell reality apart from anything else. Her perspective and mind had been so manipulated that she couldn't even recognize her face in the mirror. She often wondered whether she was alive and life was happening or whether her reality was a vivid nightmare from which she would soon wake up.

The Silent Treatment

Shunning, stonewalling, the silent treatment—whatever you want to call it, avoiding communication is a manipulative and strategic tactic intended to frustrate and alienate you.[21] A PL may refuse to speak with you or even acknowledge your existence for hours, days, or weeks. When receiving the silent treatment, you might question if or why your PL is upset and attempt to interpret messages in their behavior. Like gaslighting and love-bombing, the silent treatment controls your behaviors and thought processes.

The PL makes his victim feel rejected, alone, and unworthy by not interacting. These feelings lead you to try everything possible to regain connection with the PL. Like gaslighting, the end goal of the silent treatment is punishment. Ignoring another person is not the absence of communication—it is a vital communication of power. After being criticized, blamed, and gaslit for some time, you no longer know what to believe, but you know you can only experience positive emotions by doing things the PL's way.

Possessiveness and Jealousy

Pathological lovers are incredibly jealous even when you hang out with friends. Ironically, if they are serial cheaters, they will constantly accuse you of cheating. They do this for a few reasons. First, to keep you on the defense and distract you from their affairs. Second, they assume that if they are cheating, you might be too. Third, they don't trust other people because they think other people are selfish liars like them.[22]

When Tom and Alex were at parties, he would talk to other people yet always have one eye on Alex to keep track of whom she was interacting with. Lily went out with girlfriends one night and didn't see Jason's text before he went to sleep because her phone had died. She crawled into bed next to him a few hours later, and in the morning, he accused her of cheating. As it turns out, Jason had visited a sex worker after texting Lily goodnight and had arrived home just hours before Lily did. He was angry and stressed that he could not gauge when Lily would be home and was suspicious of her due to his new infidelity.

During the middle phase, you might try to break up with a PL due to all their crazy-making behavior. One patient told me that her PL convinced her to elope with him in Malibu during the intermediate phase after only nine months of dating. A few weeks later, it all went downhill due to his controlling behavior, emotional abuse, and vicious fights caused by his paranoid jealousy. During one battle, she left their apartment to get some air and turned off her phone, but he wouldn't stop calling her. He drove to her girlfriend's house and tried to break down the door looking for her. She decided that was it; she changed her number and left him. Then after almost a year of not speaking, she decided to call him one night after having too many drinks. He sucked her back in, and they officially married, this time for twenty years. We have worked together for several years; she has a restraining order against him and is divorcing this abusive psychopath for good.

COGNITIVE DISSONANCE

Let's answer the initial question at the beginning of this chapter, how do intelligent, loving, kind women get trapped in trauma bonds? Sandra L. Brown, MA's revolutionary research uncovered that cognitive dissonance (CD) is a significant factor. CD is an internal conflict caused by an inconsistency between your thoughts and actions. It is a normal reaction to the dual sides of Jekyll/Hyde. Just after the love-bombing stage, the PL's mask begins to slip when something he does doesn't match something you thought you knew about him. So now your whole internal thinking process starts comparing the two sides of his personas and tries to decide whether to leave or stay. Because your PL initially behaved kindly and then became controlling, you begin to see an inconsistency. You begin to have opposite relationship experiences with him.

You internally question yourself: "Do I love him or hate him?" You want to believe you can trust him, yet some of his behavior indicates that you can't. So now you feel conflicted and think, "Why am I staying with a guy I just caught lying to me?" CD is the internal thinking war that occurs as who he claims to be doesn't match his actions. As this book unfolds, you will see CD holds the trauma bond in place because it paralyzes your thinking process. It is a foundational reason why you stay bonded to a psychopath. A TBR cannot exist without CD.

The final phase of a TBR—the Last Straw—and how and why women finally leave is explained in Chapter 6 because it needs particular attention. Psychological and emotional bondage is the opposite of love. In trauma bonds, intimacy continuously depreciates, and the PL's power increases as the relationship progresses from one phase to another. Abuse slaughters you. The more intimacy depreciates, the more you experience a loss of power, a diminished sense of self, and a willingness to invest more energy to buy back love. The woman's efforts to buy back love are synonymous with giving up her needs to meet her partner's demands for power and pleasure.

Relying on anyone's love for your emotional and financial security is unhealthy. Depending on a mentally ill person is dangerous. Mature love does not ask you to sacrifice yourself. Chronic abuse, fear, and powerlessness do and are, therefore, traumatizing. This person was supposed to be your safe place for care and comfort; they are anything but. Are your close friends baffled that you, a high-functioning, bright, proactive woman, are reduced to a brainwashed version of your former self? Mind control can suck the willpower from the best of us.

We have difficulty accepting that people are deliberately cruel to each other *because* we have an emotional connection to them. (People enter trauma bonds for different reasons. Suppose you endured attachment trauma, meaning you experienced neglect and abuse in early childhood. In that case, you are at an increased risk of entering abusive adult relationships. These learned relational patterns involve feeling unlovable, longing for the closeness you never received, and fearing intimacy because it was never safe.

Yet, even healthy adults are vulnerable to trauma bonding. Therefore, trauma bonding can either be a reenactment of early relational trauma

The wheel labels, reading around:

- Deceitfulness, pathological lying; hiding things.
- Inpulsivity threatens safety and creates recklessness.
- Public image is important: it supports their power and control.
- Possessive; you are an object they are entitled to own and control.
- Twists things into opposites; manipulates and gaslights.
- Lack of insight or capacity to self-reflect.
- No remorse, empathy, compassion, or change.
- Victim mentality pulls you into their world.
- Controls access to money directly or indirectly.
- Denies or minimizes abuse.
- Constant double standards, which are abusive.
- Unhealthy values and moral compass; distorted sense of right and wrong.
- Justified in their manipulative, lying behavior.
- Entitled to being angry, dominating, and unfaithful.
- Believes they are superior.
- Isolates you from friends, family, therapist.

WHEEL OF ABUSE

Understanding Abuse

- An abuser's goals are **control** and **power**.
- Abuse is used to gain control though **fear** and **intimidation.**
- Abuse is a **learned behavior** based on values and beliefs.
- A primary outcome of abuse is to reduce a partner's power in **decision-making.**

or can suddenly be acquired in adulthood. In the aftermath of a trauma bond, there may be symptoms of cognitive dissonance, low self-esteem, lack of confidence, and a fear of ever loving again.

Whatever the cause for entering a trauma bond, we all hold on for the same reasons. Trauma bonds are like cement. PLs suck you in with their charm and love-bombing and then use coercive control and manipulation to keep you bonded. The seeds of cognitive dissonance that have been planted by the dual personas of the PL are the root of this violent attachment. The combination of intermittent abuse and power imbalance creates a cement-like grip over your heart and mind, leaving you unable to enact your own will. You stay because you feel trapped—physically, financially, psychologically, or emotionally. With traumatic bonding, women feel sorry for, empathize with, and forgive the PL, replacing and dissolving feelings of anger and entrapment.

Suppose this traumatic pattern feels familiar. In that case, the most important thing you can do to transform these patterns is to understand them. Knowledge is power. Relational patterns are learned, which means they can also be unlearned. Hear me when I say this: What was done to you was unfair and unkind. However, you and only you are responsible for changing it. Parts 2 and 3 will cover breaking free and healing from a trauma bond.

KEY POINTS TO REMEMBER

1. A trauma bond does not start abusively; it initially feels exciting, passionate, and intense.

2. Trauma bonds feature three distinct phases, each with specific behavior patterns. They are the **Sweet Seduction Phase**, the **Trauma Vortex**, and the **Last Straw**.

3. In the first phase of a trauma bond, the Sweet Seduction Phase, the PL seeks vulnerable targets, luring them in by presenting himself as charming, strong, honest, confident, interested, and dependable. He intentionally misrepresents himself and then engages in behaviors of love-bombing, intensity, mind mapping, and twinship.

4. The middle phase of a TBR, called the Trauma Vortex, begins when aspects of the PL are revealed that conflict with how he initially presented himself. During this phase, the PL becomes meaner, more dominant, and more emotionally manipulative, causing you to feel confused, submissive, powerless, and immobilized.

5. Whatever the cause for entering a trauma bond, we all hold on for the same reasons. PLs suck you in with their charm and love-bombing and then use coercive control and manipulation to keep you bonded. The survivor experiences cognitive dissonance (CD) due to the PL's words and behaviors not matching. CD is a foundational piece of the bond in TBRs.

TRAUMA BOND ASSESSMENT

1. I feel confused about our relationship because I love my partner but also fear him.

2. It's hard to leave my abusive lover because I feel emotionally or financially dependent on them.

3. My friends and family worry about my well-being in this relationship and tell me, "You don't seem like yourself."

4. My partner states he will change or do better, but he never does.

5. There is crazy-making communication that never resolves the issues in my relationship.

6. I keep hoping the fights will stop if I love better.

continued

7. I feel trapped because my partner is controlling and abusive.

8. I feel loyal to my partner even though he has harmed me.

9. I hope my partner will change once he is promoted, makes more money, reconciles with his family, etc.

10. I love how bold and fearless my partner is, though it scares me.

11. I obsessively check my partner's social media accounts and digital communications.

12. I am too embarrassed to tell my family or close friends about our fights and my partner's betrayal.

13. I have tried to leave my partner four times but keep returning.

14. I notice my partner never apologizes after emotionally abusing me.

15. I end up doing what I don't want to do to please my partner.

4 Opposites Do Attract

I can't stomach the memory any longer.

He asked me not to write about him,

Begged that I forgive his fists,

To not ruin the good name of a bad man.

I told him better you than me.[1]

—KAI-LILLY KARPMAN

TO DESIRE YOUR LOVER TO change and be repeatedly disappointed murders your soul. Every woman I have worked with during or after a trauma bond has vowed never to endure one again because the agony of cycling through hopefulness and hopelessness is excruciating. Yet, it is not enough to say you will never tolerate a TBR again. Many well-intentioned women have said this, read books, and engaged in therapy, only to find themselves puzzled when they fall into the arms of another pathological partner. The secret ingredient in the recipe of relational health is understanding your personality. I implore you to read this chapter slowly, take your time, and soak it in to understand the personality traits which make you vulnerable to traumatic bonding.

CODEPENDENCY

Before I go into the specifics of women's personalities, I want to address a personal pet peeve. We must stop labeling every woman who endures abuse as "enabling" or "codependent." In the 1980s, Codependents Anonymous meetings were created to support people related to or living with an alcoholic or addict who tolerated and enabled their highly dysfunctional behavior. Codependents Anonymous does not officially define a codependent person but lists various behavior patterns. The inability to define codependency is telling.

The codependency movement was made hugely popular by Melody Beattie, a survivor of an alcoholic home. Beattie describes codependency as caretaking, low self-worth, repressed feelings, obsessing over things, denial, dependency, weak boundaries, poor communication, need to control, lack of trust, anger, and sexual problems.[2] Ironically, these are the same symptoms evident in traumatized individuals— which makes sense when you understand that living with an addict or alcoholic is a traumatizing experience.

Codependency contains a broad category of behaviors many people have. Beattie's list is unscientific and has never been connected to any *DSM* diagnosis. A few attempts to measure codependency as a personality disorder fizzled out, as it proved as slippery as a horoscope. Indeed, there is no reliable research support for "codependency." However, in recent years, Beattie's proposed characteristics have been associated with symptoms of Complex PTSD.

Codependency eventually infiltrated domestic violence language. The concept of codependency has become part of family counseling, which is why therapists have labeled many abuse victims with codependency. Women have traditionally been caregivers in society; pop psychology turned their traditional nurturing role into a "disorder" riddled with shame.

Codependent people are said to be those who stop the addict from hitting the clichéd bottom. However, first, pathological lovers (PL) don't hit bottom because they have a monopoly on power; they abuse their partners at home and in private, and they get away with murder (figuratively and literally). They may scratch the bottom when they get hit with a restraining order against them, yet they don't always respect the order and find ways to bend the rules. Law enforcement and the family court system often fall prey to the PL's manipulative tactics and become complicit in their abusive ploys—yet we don't slap them with the codependent title.

Second, why would any sane person want to enable someone to abuse and lie to them? Abuse and exploitation are always wrong, regardless of whether you're an insecure, naive, trusting, or healthy human being. Nobody deserves to be abused—period! Abusers toss around the word "codependency" because it offloads blame onto their victims. And they are expert blamers.

Pathological lovers are blamers; they scream that you'll never grow and heal unless you "accept responsibility" for your role in the dynamic (because it takes two to tango, blah blah blah). Here's the truth: it's perfectly possible to recover, grow, and become whole without accepting responsibility for someone else's toxic and cruel behavior. Any halfway decent therapist who cares about their patient would feel pain in seeing her suffer and want to alleviate the suffering instead of simply boxing her into a codependency diagnosis. When a victim finally realizes it's not her, it's him, she starts to set boundaries. She discovers his excuses are all lies that have nothing to do with intimacy. The only thing victims are responsible for is examining why and how they got into an abusive situation in the first place and, if there are kids involved, protecting them from being abused too. Now that I have cleared up codependency, let us explore why certain personalities are primed to end up in a trauma bond.

THE BIG FIVE PERSONALITY TRAITS OF THE SURVIVOR

It's hard to understand just how much personality impacts our lives. We know certain things about ourselves, such as, "I'm outgoing, low maintenance, organized, and trusting," but we rarely consider personality beyond the most obvious traits. We have lived with our personality from birth, so it doesn't produce as much curiosity as our changing mood. We aren't curious about our specific personality traits and their intensity until we recognize a pattern of repeatedly dating the same type of person—and usually, we have been tortured by their empty promises and our frustration.

Many misguided theories exist about why women enter and stay in TBRs. These incorrect assumptions are why survivors have been wrongfully labeled codependent or co-perpetrators. Not enough attention has been paid to how survivors' personalities influence their relationships. Hence, stigmatizing labels such as learned helplessness, low self-esteem, and love addiction are assumed to be the reasons for women's engagement with TBRs. Thankfully, Sandra L. Brown, MA, and her team have discovered an educated explanation.

Sandra L. Brown, MA, conducted thirty years of research on the personality traits of female victims of trauma bonds. Using the 2007 Temperament Character Inventory and the 2014 five-factor model rating form (FFM), she discovered that many domestic violence survivors have two elevated personality traits: conscientiousness and agreeableness.[3,4]

In the FFM, each personality trait defines how a person tends to think, feel, behave, and become motivated. Personality traits are measured by how they are expressed, from very low to very high. Unlike mood, which changes daily, personality endures throughout the lifespan.

Whereas personality traits are basic tendencies that do not change, habits, attitudes, and behaviors are how we express personality and adapt to our current environment, so these things can and do change. For example, a woman who scores high in conscientiousness is high

Five Factor Model Personality Traits

OPENNESS

Describes flexible thinking, active imagination, sensitivity to aesthetics, deep awareness of feelings and readiness to reexamine social and political values.

Features:
fantasy
aesthetics
feelings
actions
ideas
values

CONSCIENTIOUSNESS

Describes tendency to think before acting, take responsibility, be hardworking, orderly and ethical.

Features:
competence
order
dutifulness
achievement
striving
self-discipline
deliberation

EXTRAVERSION

Describe strong desire for social attention and connection, tendency to exhibit dominant behavior, have high energy, and feel positive emotions.

Features:
warmth
gregariousness
assertiveness
activity
excitement-seeking
positive emotions

AGREEABLENESS

Describes motivation to maintain positive harmonious connections with others, tendency toward being trusting, honest, humble, forgiving, sympathetic and empathetic.

Features:
trust
straightforwardness
altruism
compliance
modesty
tendermindedness

NEUROTICISM

Describe tendency toward feeling anxious, angry, depressed, and embarassed, as well as the inability to control cravings and urges.

Features:
anxiety
anger-hostility
depression
self-consciousness
impulsiveness
vulnerability

functioning, driven, and has integrity, so she will thrive in a stable and balanced environment. Placing that same woman in an unstable and threatening atmosphere will prompt her to abandon her integrity for survival and hinder her ability to excel—her habits, attitudes, and behaviors will change. She'll go to therapy because nothing seems to be going right, and now she is depressed. Still, she is depressed due to her pathological partnership. She is not going to heal herself from being a conscious person, nor should she! She will heal by honoring and embracing her moral, conscientious nature and removing the people or things that stand in the way of allowing her to live authentically. When her environment is stable and balanced again, her depression ceases, and she is free to excel. Understanding how a woman's innate personality traits of conscientiousness and agreeableness make her a trauma bond magnet is essential. We'll begin with agreeableness because this trait blinds women to the initial TBR red flags.

If you would like to assess your Big Five traits, go to the site brain-manager.io and click on the personality test. The assessment has 300 questions, costs $1.00, and takes about twenty minutes.

The brain manager website will then email you your results within two hours.

High Agreeableness

Agreeableness is the personality trait that motivates a woman to maintain positive, harmonious connections with others. Therefore, it makes sense that such women are described as peacekeeping, softhearted, easygoing, trustworthy, honest, tolerant, and empathetic. In relationships, they are humble, helpful, cooperative, and emotionally sensitive to others' needs. An agreeable woman is naturally selfless and eager to calm others. Because they are trusting and good-natured, they never second-guess anyone. The value they place on connection mixes with their drive to maintain harmony and bestows upon them a double-edged sword of forgiving and forgetting quickly. They are the opposite of an antagonistic lover; agreeable women are true lovers.

Keri and Alex scored very high in agreeableness. Both bent to the will of their PL when it came to their careers and friendships, and both went above and beyond to appease their PLs, especially when abuse and betrayal were rampant.

Under the umbrella of **agreeableness** are the features of *trust*, *straightforwardness*, *altruism*, *compliance*, *modesty*, and *tender-mindedness*.[5]

TRUST

To trust someone is to believe they are honest, safe, and reliable. A trusting woman is well-intentioned and sincere, and she believes in the goodness of others. She does not have a suspicious nature, so she doesn't think that trust must be earned. Sandra L. Brown, MA, states that out of all the features of agreeableness, the woman's trusting nature allows her PL to seduce and harm her quickly because harm is the furthest thing from her mind.[6]

Her optimistic perspective on human nature has served her in her past relationships. She likely has long-term harmonious relationships with friends from childhood, high school, or employment. Because she is trustworthy, she thinks most people are loyal and faithful, so she lacks lie-telling and detection skills. The trusting woman is slow to judge, giving others the benefit of the doubt. She cares about the quality of her relationships because they are the primary source of her happiness. Some people desire to invest in stocks, but she likes to invest in her relationships. Sandra L. Brown, MA, calls agreeableness the "relationship investment trait."[7] Nothing in her belief system or relationship experiences would imply she needs to be wary of an admirer who initially adores her—until she gets crushed by a psychopath. Yet, even then, she finds it challenging to wrap her head around the reality that a person could be so cruel.

Trusting women are super responsive to seduction because seduction implies emotional closeness, which they value deeply. When her partner shares his innermost thoughts and feelings, she assumes he is being authentic and vulnerable, not pretending to be her soulmate. So, when he says, "Your love has saved my life," as Tom said to Alex, or "I haven't had the urge to gamble since meeting you," as Larry said to Juno, she is naturally bonded.

The PL leads the trusting woman to believe she is safe with him, so of course, she gradually comes to depend on him. Naively, she dismisses his lies. He begs her forgiveness when the truth comes out—"I was stupid! I will never cheat again!"—and she believes him. She forgives, forgets, and moves on, hoping he can change because she thinks he is like her. Hope is her hook.

Trust holds our society together. It cements relationships, allowing people to live and love. Being trusting is, therefore, a prosocial quality. Imagine a world without any transparent, sincere, and authentic people. Life would suck! The problem is not her. It's him. His intentional lies make her optimistic, yet her positive outlook sabotages her. Remember the invisible ship theory: She doesn't realize she is being tricked until she is trapped. Lacking threat detection skills, she trusts untrustworthy suitors. She is perfect prey for a manipulative lover focused only on meeting his emotional, sexual, and financial needs.

STRAIGHTFORWARDNESS

Straightforward individuals are honest. Sincere people know authentic communication is the best way to connect. However, transparency with a PL is dangerous. The PL will initially parrot a straightforward woman's genuine feelings, leading her to believe she has met her soulmate. Overdisclosing her values and insecurities gives him a window to her soul, making her easier to control. Transparency and her overly trusting nature give him an arsenal of exploitable information. Recall that on their first date, Lily revealed to Jason the importance of going to therapy. He hooked her by saying he loved the treatment and that it had helped him tremendously. From that moment on, attending therapy and appearing to be "doing the work" became a highly effective strategy for him to prey on Lily.

ALTRUISM

Another word for love is altruism. A generous person is tender and has a solid moral compass, which guides them to value and be concerned for others' well-being. And due to their selfless nature, they enjoy being of service.

Loving-kindness and compassion are the two faces of altruism: loving-kindness wants your lover to experience happiness; compassion focuses on soothing his suffering—both beautiful intentions. While the altruistic person is focused on others' pleasure, a PL is fixated on his own. So, he will unflinchingly do whatever makes him feel good. Since he is without compassion, he will refuse to answer questions or offer explanations. He's also insensitive after you tell him how hurtful it is when he insults and gaslights you. An altruistic woman's selfless nature causes her to abandon herself and her dignity in the name of love, as Juno did when she lied to the police about Larry's abuse to keep him safe.

According to Sandra L. Brown, MA, women tolerate men's insults because they have positive memory intrusion.[8] Intrusive memories are a common feature of post-traumatic stress disorder (PTSD), and they come from involuntary thoughts, flashbacks, and nightmares. People often assume intrusive memories derive only from harmful events, but they can result from happy occasions too. Someone with a prosocial personality is sentimental; their brain delivers images of the intoxicating beginning filled with roses, affection, and compliments even as problems arise. She goes down a sentimental spiral and is flooded with memories of the good moments, quickly forgetting the hard and painful ones and prioritizing the positive. Positive memory intrusion intensifies the positive, making it difficult to face reality and move on once the relationship ends.

COMPLIANCE

This feature of agreeableness concerns interpersonal conflict. High scorers tend to be cooperative peacekeepers. Compliant people are accommodating because their end goal is social harmony. If a woman scores high in compliance, she understands the assignment in intimacy is to be pro-relationship. All relationships have cycles of fighting and making up. Yet a cooperative woman is motivated to accommodate her PL to maintain peace. When her partner emotionally triggers her, her desire to eliminate drama motivates her to control (minimize) her emotions and de-escalate the fight. Also, she is sensitive to her lover's pain so that she can be flexible and adaptive in conflict—but this also leaves her open to becoming her lover's doormat.

When assaulted with cruel insults, such as "You would be nothing without me" or "You're a useless waste of a human," she can stay calm and not retaliate. Survivors are kind, so antagonism and hostility are not the first cards they pull out when in conflict. When her PL physically harms her, she wants to avoid drama and negative consequences, so she doesn't call the police. Instead, she uses all her energy to defuse her lover's fury. After her husband threw their daughter into the car's trunk, Keri hadn't considered legal action until I brought it up in session.

The woman whose PL is possessive and rageful learns to comply to avoid his wrath. She doesn't want to be controlled, yet continuously fighting about going out for a night or having a weekend getaway with her friends is exhausting, so she stays home—like Keri did when Nick raged. While intimate partner violence professionals link these traits to learned helplessness or codependency, they don't realize that being accommodating stems from your innate personality. It is important to note that the FFM describes compliance as being more about your open attitude and flexible responsiveness and less about conforming.

MODESTY

Modesty describes how we relate to ourselves, our strengths, and our limitations. It involves how we place ourselves among others and the world at large. Individuals who score high in modesty are humble and do not need to be the center of attention. However, they do not necessarily lack self-confidence.

Modesty is the opposite of entitlement. Modest women will put others' needs first because they do not consider themselves superior. They enjoy being generous with their time and attention when helping others. They hold the belief that "there is plenty to go around."

Arrogant PLs think they are the bee's knees and will relentlessly boast about themselves. Modest women don't rank themselves as better or worse because they know we are all equal. Humble women are not grandiose; they accurately appraise their strengths and weaknesses.

TENDER-MINDEDNESS

Tender-mindedness measures sympathy, empathy, and concern for others. High scorers are deeply affected by their partner's emotions. Empathy refers to the ability "to feel the other from within." Tender-minded individuals emotionally resonate with others. A PL manipulates his partner's empathy to advance his agenda while keeping his partner glued to his side. Recall Juno, who stuck it out with Larry after he threatened suicide when she caught him cheating, or Lily, who continued forgiving Jason's betrayals as he revealed more of his childhood pain to her.

Empathy cements a woman to her PL because she can instantly put herself in his shoes. She empathizes with his past pain and overlooks his devilishness, like Alex, who forgave Tom's betrayals repeatedly as he played on her compassion. Her genetic disposition for hyper-empathy and innocent nature looks like codependency to therapists who are not experts in trauma bonds.

A tender-minded woman resonates with her PL's pain. And her compassion makes her want to alleviate his suffering. She wants to solve his problem and heal his shame—or at least be the one standing by his side when he does so for himself. So, she gives him unconditional love while he unconditionally controls her. She desires to cure his childhood wounds. When he doesn't change, she blames herself for not being helpful enough. And she sticks around, convinced he needs a little more time. But she is not his mother; she is his lover.

The PL understands his partner is highly empathetic, so he tries to evoke her pity and compassion by victim signaling. Even though PLs are frequently hostile and angry, they often claim to be victimized. A kind person naturally wants to relieve her partner's pain. Alex and Lily believed their lovers when they said their last girlfriends were mean, lied, cheated, and put them down. Alex and Lily became caretakers to compensate for Tom's and Jason's prior romantic disappointments. They thought they could help their PLs overcome their problems and realize their potential with enough love, patience, and dedication. Due to their empathic nature, they hated to see their lovers suffer, so they slowly sacrificed their well-being to boost their PLs'.

Combining a PL with a woman whose innate temperament drives her to reduce conflict, elevate harmony, and be tolerant illuminates why she gets stuck in intermittent cycles of abuse. Scoring high on the FFM's trait of agreeableness paves the way for a predatory PL to prey on the selfless, trusting, and optimistic woman. Her prosocial personality and belief that people are inherently good blind her to the PL's dangerous, antisocial personality.

Her agreeableness makes her vulnerable to being targeted and trauma bonded. Because she sees others as she sees herself, her loyalty and hopefulness keep her hooked once she has become attached to him—even when his pathology harms her emotionally, physically, and financially. Sadly, the PL takes a personality trait that usually creates healthy bonds and twists it into a torturous characteristic.

High Conscientiousness

According to Sandra L. Brown, MA, a TBR survivor's next elevated personality trait is conscientiousness, which she defines as an "integrity-oriented life" trait.[9] We know that high-functioning women end up in trauma bonds because their high agreeableness blinds them to the PL's false charms. So why can't they leave, or why didn't they leave sooner? Their high-to-normal conscientiousness explains this.

Conscientious women are governed by their conscience; this means they are aware of what's right and wrong and tend to follow social norms. Conscientiousness is the trait that makes one capable and good at organizing and planning. A highly conscientious woman is reflective and thinks before acting, which makes her the opposite of her impulsive partner.

Women scoring high-normal on conscientiousness are very responsible and perseverant because they take their obligations seriously. They possess good morals due to their prosocial ethics. Maintaining standards of excellence often makes them workaholics and perfectionists. Their persistence pays off, and such women make excellent students and excel in demanding careers. Yet all these quali-ties, which make them determined to reach their goals in life, also make them committed to achieving their goals in love and keep them entangled in the PL's web. Keri, Alex, and Lily all score incredibly high in conscientiousness.

Under the umbrella of conscientiousness are the features of *competence, order, dutifulness, achievement, striving, self-discipline,* and *deliberation.* Women who often find themselves as victims of PLs score strongly in these categories. They are excellent problem-solvers, value order over chaos, uphold responsibility and are reliable, have high aspi-rations and work hard to achieve their goals, know their values and core beliefs, and intentionally plan their lives and focus on the future.

WOMEN WITH DEPENDENT PERSONALITY DISORDER

Joshua D. Miller is an American psychologist, personality researcher, and expert on the Dark Tetrad. In a conversation with him, he expressed how anyone and everyone can fall prey to a toxic Casanova. I agree with him. Yet, through my study of Sandra L. Brown, MA's research and my years of clinical practice, I have witnessed two other types of women with specific personality traits that get trapped in trauma bonds. Those with a dependent personality and women with a history of early developmental trauma. So, in this section, I illumi-nate their personality traits so you can see which category you may fall into. Remember that understanding your personality is a way to avoid these smooth operators.

A TBR is a social trap, especially if you have a dependent personal-ity disorder (DPD) or traits included in this diagnosis. A woman with DPD has an excessive need to be cared for, leading to submissive and clingy behavior. Such women deeply dread rejection and separation from those they are bonded to. These women have an underdeveloped sense of independence; thus, their lovers are their lifeline. However, the PL is not a lifeboat but a tidal wave that causes the need for a lifeboat.

Women with DPD are insecure. These individuals tend to be passive and allow other people (typically one other person) to take the initiative and assume responsibility for the most significant areas of their lives. These women are panicked about abandonment because they feel helpless and struggle to manage themselves and their well-being. Hence, they desperately need others. And relational tensions threaten their lifeline, so they avoid conflict.

Due to their lack of confidence, these women become paralyzed when making decisions. They ask for everyone's advice, which disconnects them from their authenticity. These women are generally overdependent on the people closest to them.

In all TBRs, the PL exploits his partner's love and trust to satisfy his needs for status, power, and pleasure. A highly dependent woman can get seduced and conned due to her personality traits. I have all my patients take the 240-question five-factor model and consistently see the following pattern in DPD women:

- High to very high agreeableness (high trust, altruism, compliance, tender-mindedness, and modesty)
- Low conscientiousness (low competence and self-discipline)
- High neuroticism (high anxiousness, depressiveness, vulnerability, and self-consciousness)[10]

These traits and personalities make these women prime victims of coercive control. When their TBR ends, women with DPD are devastated and go to extremes to obtain care and compassion from others, including sleeping with strangers, overwhelming their friends, and returning to their abusers (or finding new abusers). Although their PLs tortured them, these women fantasized that their abusers might still return to save them. Larry got Juno arrested and stripped her of everything. After all this, in one session, she said, "Larry will realize he made a mistake and come back one day." Another patient who found out her husband of over twenty years had molested their daughters in childhood struggled with longing for him for several years after their divorce. Women with DPD often suffer from "toxic amnesia."

Without a professional understanding of their motives and personality traits, survivors will be misdiagnosed with depression, codependency, and social anxiety. Women and therapists cannot treat properly when there is a misdiagnosis. Understanding yourself and your PL's personality and tactics will make you aware of why you endured a TBR, so you can be an active participant in your recovery and ensure you never suffer a TBR again.

WOMEN WITH COMPLEX POST-TRAUMATIC STRESS DISORDER (C-PTSD)

I have worked with countless survivors of chronic childhood abuse and neglect. Many women who sought my help recovering from a trauma bond had a diagnosis of C-PTSD before their relationship. In this section, I will explain the common personality traits that women with trauma histories have that cause them to become trauma bonded.

C-PTSD is generated by adverse childhood experiences (ACEs), which include abuse and neglect, where abuse is the addition of a detrimental element and neglect is the lack of a necessary component. ACEs include emotional abuse (being humiliated, judged, criticized, insulted, controlled, or manipulated), physical abuse (non-accidental bodily harm), and sexual abuse (being forcefully touched, kissed, molested, or violated). ACEs include emotional neglect (being ignored, disregarded, having feelings or experiences denied or minimized, lacking compassion) and physical neglect (insufficient shelter, safety, clothing, or food). The result of chronic adverse experiences is a child who feels deeply ashamed, insecure, and untrusting of others.[11]

C-PTSD sets the stage for lifelong struggles with depression, anxiety, and relationship issues. We learn about empathy and connection from our earliest relationships—the relationship we share with our parents or caretakers. The little girl who experiences abuse or neglect in her earliest relationships grows into a woman who believes love includes abuse and neglect. She is at a relational and emotional disadvantage and struggles to choose healthy love because she knows no such thing. Instead, she gravitates toward partners whose love feels familiar with the quality of care they received in childhood, and their cycle of trauma repeats until she breaks out of her trance like Sleeping Beauty.

The attachment these women shared with their parents was a toxic combination of hostility, love, and feeling hopeful things would improve. Sound familiar? You got it—intermittent abuse. Now, as adults, having been bonded to parents who were 85 percent rejecting and 15 percent gratifying, these women have a high chance of entering a trauma bond. As grown-ups, they believe "love" is defined by intermittent care rather than consistent experiences of being accepted and treasured. Therefore, their partner is both their tormentor and security. They associate love with feeling hopeful their lover will change, only to be abused or neglected by him again. Sadly, these women learned as children that intimate attachment does not include consistency, trust, or empathy. Early relational trauma directly affects adult romantic relationships.

Growing up in a chronically abusive or neglectful environment—mainly as their personality develops—leaves them with long-lasting impacts. These women's most common personality traits are **high conscientiousness** and **low agreeableness**. They might see the PL's red flags, but their deep yearning for love and connection (which they did not get in childhood) turns those red flags into pink flags. And once they're in, boy, it's mission impossible for them to get out.

High Conscientiousness

In my practice, the women who endured ACEs scored high in conscientiousness—specifically, achievement striving and self-discipline. As children, they lived in chaos and terror. The one person they could rely on was themselves, and the one thing they learned they could control was their goals. A primary symptom of C-PTSD is shame. Becoming a high-achieving person is an effective way to offset feelings of inadequacy and worthlessness.

This woman's overachieving nature inevitably saves her because she values her work, education, and personal pursuits. In a trauma bond, her body experiences high stress levels. However, she cannot truly sense her high stress as she is used to handling high-conflict situations. After all, chaos was her usual. Thus, because she can manage more than most, she thinks the same is true in her romantic life. When Jason admitted he was addicted to porn and received validation from dating apps and chat rooms, major alarms should have gone off in Lily's head. Instead, she viewed his behavior as a problem she could help him fix, even if it cost her sleepless nights and weekly panic attacks.

However, Lily's self-discipline helped her maintain some self-esteem, which kept her anchored when her relationship became chaotic. Despite the emotional abuse and psychological torment she experienced from Jason, she had a strong work ethic and continued to excel in school. This boosted her confidence and provided something on which she could focus her energy aside from him. The highly conscientious woman garners self-esteem from her accomplishments. When a TBR threatens her goals, she will exhaust all possible options to maintain her lover and her life before deciding to leave. Once she is worn down, she will not let anyone interfere with the one reliable resource which has helped her survive—herself.

Low Agreeableness

Under the trait of low agreeableness, these women score very low in trust and compliance but, on average, high in tender-mindedness. Not surprisingly, women who have been abused or neglected by those who were supposed to protect them (parents) do not trust others easily. So, how can they be seduced into a TBR if they are untrusting?

Because they believe people generally can't be trusted, they think they have a sixth sense for psychopaths. Lily got caught in an abuser's web before she realized the web even existed. The good news is that, if this is you, the information in this book will likely help you sharpen your sixth sense.

Abused women with C-PTSD are sometimes called co-perpetrators because they are perceived as incredibly high-functioning, so how could they unknowingly experience such deception? Yet, due to her low compliance or low obedience, the target believes she is immune to manipulation.

These ladies tend to react angrily to the abuse. They are argumentative and aggressive, which creates the illusion that they hold power in their dynamic and that they can handle a PL. Such women also react to abuse with "violent resistance." Violent resistance is aggression in response to being abused, controlled, and dominated. They get reactively angry when they need to defend or protect themselves.[12] And what makes the PL's abuse different is their motivation to have control over their lover. Her violence arises in reaction to the multiple strands that the PL uses to dominate her.

On the surface, violent resistance can look like mutual abuse—if no one investigates who's initiating the abuse and who's in control. Mutual abuse is also called situational couple violence, but it isn't domestic violence. This abuse happens among people with poor conflict resolution skills. When such couples talk about whether to go on vacation or buy a car, they engage in mutual low-level hostile communication. Unlike

IPV, this abuse is not driven by the need to exert power over another or control them.

Even though these women's average scores in agreeableness are low, they all scored average to high in tender-mindedness. Tender-mindedness measures attitudes of sympathy and concern for others; they can relate to what others are feeling. Lily scored high in tendermindedness, and Jason weaponized her kindness and sympathy for him. Whenever Jason was caught lying to or cheating on Lily, he pulled on her heartstrings by belittling and criticizing himself. His self-pity elicited compassion and understanding from her, which kept her trauma bonded to him.

A TBR can be a reactivation or reliving of early attachment experiences. The brain wants familiarity; the root word "fam" means one's people. The PL's coercive control, selfishness, dominant threats, and neglect of their emotional needs feel familiar to the women because this is what they experienced growing up. Women with C-PTSD associate love with chaos because chaos is where they've learned to function best. Thus, their PLs, unfortunately, feel like home instead of a war zone.

PATRIARCHY

Our patriarchal culture also shapes our identities and what we consider acceptable in our relationships. We are fed messages through songs, movies, advertisements, and literature depicting socially created norms about women's roles in romantic love. Romantic comedies routinely show two mismatched people who conquer difficult obstacles to find lasting love. The woman is always a lovely beauty with everything going for her. He is often beastlike, with major hang-ups before she transforms him into the man of her dreams. The courtship is bumpy, but their dream of living happily ever after is their prize, made possible mainly by her selfless efforts. Because, of course, "true love conquers all." However, many depictions of romantic love are

Victim/Survivor Five-Factor Traits

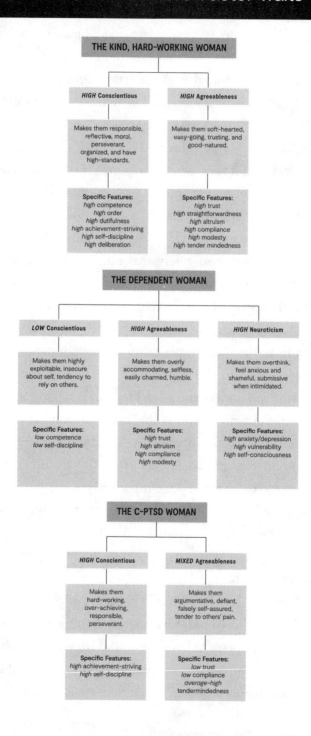

THE KIND, HARD-WORKING WOMAN

HIGH Conscientious

Makes them responsible, reflective, moral, perseverant, organized, and have high-standards.

Specific Features:
high competence
high order
high dutifulness
high achievement-striving
high self-discipline
high deliberation

HIGH Agreeableness

Makes them soft-hearted, easy-going, trusting, and good-natured.

Specific Features:
high trust
high straightforwardness
high altruism
high compliance
high modesty
high tender mindedness

THE DEPENDENT WOMAN

LOW Conscientious

Makes them highly exploitable, insecure about self, tendency to rely on others.

Specific Features:
low competence
low self-discipline

HIGH Agreeableness

Makes them overly accommodating, selfless, easily charmed, humble.

Specific Features:
high trust
high altruism
high compliance
high modesty

HIGH Neuroticism

Makes them overthink, feel anxious and shameful, submissive when intimidated.

Specific Features:
high anxiety/depression
high vulnerability
high self-consciousness

THE C-PTSD WOMAN

HIGH Conscientious

Makes them hard-working, over-achieving, responsible, perseverant.

Specific Features:
high achievement-striving
high self-discipline

MIXED Agreeableness

Makes them argumentative, defiant, falsely self-assured, tender to others' pain.

Specific Features:
low trust
low compliance
average-high tendermindedness

not healthy examples, which sets women up to fall prey to PLs and traumatic bonding.

The patriarchy is a social system created and perpetuated by males. In a patriarchal system, one person has power over another.[13] This hierarchal concept can be traced back to males from the dawn of time. Certain men who abuse this hierarchal system have laid a solid foundation for TBRs.

Not long ago, a wife was considered her husband's property and had no legal rights. In the 1980s, new laws against marital rape recognized that men had no right to demand sex from their wives whenever they wanted. Before 1980, sexual consent was considered a given on the wedding day and never canceled.

Today, we still live in a society that ranks women below men at every level, from the home and boardroom to our government. This subordination happens even in the courtroom, as we often see. Harvard psychiatrist Judith Herman wrote, "The legal system is designed to protect men from the state's superior power but not to protect women or children from the superior power of men."[14] Indeed, any TBR survivor reading this will understand what Herman is talking about.

I looked up the term "family court" online. I came across this definition: "The organization representing children in the courts." The online definition couldn't be further from the truth. I witness my patients having to behave 100 percent perfectly in the eyes of the court while their ex-husbands still lie and manipulate their way through the court system. This legal organization still clearly benefits men, and the number of times I have witnessed this truth in my patients' lives could fill a library all its own.

When Alex was looking for an attorney, a high-profile celebrity attorney told her she would have to "go through the motions, go through the steps in place in the system, and try not to be emotional." This lawyer told a woman whose children were abused and beaten in front of her not to be "emotional" while fighting to protect herself and her children from further abuse. So, her journey began. She told me, "I finally dared to leave an abusive relationship and save my children. I was told not to be emotional and had no choice but to go through a system not equipped to understand or deal with the pathology of a psychopathic ex-partner and father." A father can appear to be a good man to the courts yet still torture his wife throughout the divorce process.

I watched Alex's abuse continue (despite a restraining order), financially and legally, not to mention her ex-partner's efforts to isolate her from friends and family. Tom was court-ordered to pay her alimony and child support, and for five months, he didn't. He was almost rewarded when he exhibited "normal" behavior, such as finally paying child support for one month. It seemed all his despicable behavior had been forgotten. Tom had supervised visits with a court-ordered monitor whom he would incessantly call and harass to the point she quit. When he blocked Alex from using her bank accounts or harassed their child's court-appointed monitor, Alex was forced to remain calm to avoid appearing as the "crazy, unfit mother." The court consistently did not restrain him, yet Tom's crazy behavior continued to control Alex from afar. The court instead penalized Alex for stepping out of line in mere milliseconds, repeatedly catered to the perpetrator's needs, and ignored the victim, her terrorized child, and what was best for them. In the end, the court seemed more concerned with appeasing Tom than doing what was right. A pathological person is so conniving that they can manipulate the legal system and its minions into behaving exactly how they want. The family court system is suited for straightforward, low-conflict divorces. It is not prepared to handle cases of intimate partner violence or trauma bond divorces, and indeed not dark, pathological personalities.

Unfortunately, this is the sad state of our court system. We label women as having learned helplessness and codependency if they do not leave a harmful situation. Then when they do, with fewer resources, less income, responsibility for caretaking, no protection, and fighting for their lives, their children are thrown into the lion's den: the family court system. Women are forced to ascend through several rings of hell before they can think about their own needs or immerse themselves in their healing. Sometimes this takes two years. Sometimes, it takes upwards of ten. And by the time it's all said and done, the PL has usually bled his former partner dry.

With the advent of neuroscience, personality assessments, and brain imaging, there is no longer any excuse for believing that all parents should share custody simply because they provided DNA. The family court is an outdated institution riddled with old patriarchal values. Whoever has the most resources or is the best amoral liar can dominate, exploit, and control the other.

Men abuse women because society teaches men they are entitled to anything and anyone. Western culture implies that if men do not have power, they won't succeed—they won't get the girl and make money. They will be vulnerable to other men's violence and control. Failing to assert themselves like "real men," they will be poor, alone, and unwanted —a humiliating social death that feels literal to most men.

Many PLs who have experienced attachment trauma in childhood develop another layer of entitlement, further complicating this matter. Perpetrators who were dominated and controlled in childhood vow never to let this happen again. Trauma-based entitlement is very common in abusive people—the perception of "I had to go through so much, so you must deal with whatever I do to you. Life isn't fair." When this entitlement is questioned, they experience deep humiliation. PLs who feel threatened in response to their control being challenged are likelier to lash out. When insecurity, toxic shame, and entitlement combine, these create "humiliated fury."[15] Combining a severely pathological individual's humiliated fury with the idea that women should prioritize others' needs gives you the perfect scenario for TBR.

Remember that a trauma-bonded woman is trapped by her circumstances, not her character. And people enter trauma bonds for different reasons. Suppose you endured early attachment trauma; in that case, your learned relational patterns of feeling unlovable, longing for closeness, and fearing intimacy can feel familiar.

Yet, even healthy adults are vulnerable to trauma bonding. Sandra L. Brown, MA's research illuminated that many women lured into a traumatic attachment did not have early developmental trauma. They entered because of a personality proclivity, and the PL targeted their agreeableness and conscientiousness. Because the PL knew he could exploit her kindness and integrity. And all the women had normal to very high tender-mindedness; they were concerned for others and had empathy. The PL weaponized their partner's prosocial traits against them so he could meet his needs for money, power, pleasure, and status. So please, can everyone stop blaming the survivor?

Therefore, trauma bonding can either be a reenactment of early relational trauma or can suddenly be acquired in adulthood. During and after a trauma bond, you will experience trauma symptoms, which will be explained in Chapter 5.

Suppose you are in or have survived a TBR. In that case, I implore you to have your personality tested using the five-factor model to understand your personality traits. On page 86 is a web address to take this test.

Hear me when I say this: Clinicians cannot help patients recover while looking at IPV through dated theoretical lenses. Therapists cannot treat what they don't recognize. Do not waste your precious time and money paying for a professional who is not an expert in pathological love relationships.

KEY POINTS TO REMEMBER

1. Codependency: Codependents Anonymous does not officially define a codependent person but instead lists various behavior patterns. Codependency is not an official diagnosis. A few

attempts to measure codependency as a personality disorder fizzled out.

2. Women with high agreeableness and high conscientiousness

     a. Highly agreeable women are trusting, straightforward, altruistic, compliant (peacekeeping), modest (humble), and tender-minded (empathetic). These inherent personality traits make her blind to a PL's red flags from the outset.

     b. Highly conscientious women are competent, making them expert problem-solvers; they value order, which motivates them to resolve chaos by any means; they are dutiful, which makes them responsible; they are achievement-strivers, which makes them resourceful, driven, and devoted; and they are self-disciplined and deliberate, fueling them to ride out the storm for long-term gains. High conscientiousness explains why women cannot leave trauma bonds or stay for longer than they should.

3. Women with dependent personality disorder score high in agreeableness, low in conscientiousness, and high in neuroticism.

4. Women with complex post-traumatic stress disorder (C-PTSD)

     a. C-PTSD is generated by adverse childhood experiences (ACEs), which include abuse and neglect. The little girl who experiences abuse or neglect in her earliest relationships grows into a woman who believes love includes abuse and neglect.

     b. The woman with C-PTSD scores high in conscientiousness, which makes her achievement striving. And she scores low in agreeableness (very low in trust and compliance, but average to high in tender-mindedness), which creates the illusion that she cannot be manipulated, causes her to lash out in self-defensive anger when she is harmed, and makes her tender to her lover's pain.

5. Patriarchy is a social system created and perpetuated by males. In a patriarchal system, one person has power over another. Today, we still live in a society that ranks women below men at every level, from the home and boardroom to our government. This type of system makes it easier for male PLs to survive and thrive.

PART 2

Trauma Bond Free

5 | Emotional Scar Tissue

> None have been more profound for our purposes in understanding trauma bonding than the redefining of post-traumatic stress disorder, or PTSD. Initially revolutionary in helping to understand the woundedness caused by trauma, its primary focus has been on the anxiety and fear that haunts the life of the exploited or abused victim.[1]
>
> **—PATRICK CARNES**

I OFTEN EXPLAIN THAT THERAPY with my patients in a traumatic attachment is similar to doing emotional triage work in an emergency room. Survivors are casualties of lethal love. This section aims to encourage a compassionate understanding of your trauma symptoms. As you read this chapter, notice what trauma symptoms you are experiencing because, in the last section of this book, I offer tools and action plans to manage and heal your symptoms.

IPV victims have typically been characterized by *learned helplessness*. Positive psychologist Martin Seligman coined the term after extensive research on human behavior at the University of Pennsylvania.[2] The learned helplessness theory states that abuse victims stay bonded to their perpetrators because mistreatment instills fear into them. As the abuse continues, the victim becomes psychologically paralyzed and feels powerless. Learned helplessness was applied in the cases of abused women in the 1970s to explain why women stay in trauma bonds. While the intention was good, I believe the term is somewhat shaming and disempowering to victims. Thus, I prefer the alternative term: active survivor (AS).[3]

An active survivor is an abused woman who creatively and bravely develops coping strategies to reduce the severity of her abuse. Even while experiencing severe psychological impairment, such as depression, many trauma-bonded women seek help, adapt, and try to love while enduring one. As sufferers of coercive control, they try to protect themselves and their children by making the best of an unstable situation.

The AS submits to their partner's demands to keep some peace and semblance of normalcy. Tom's road rage and reckless driving terrorized Alex. One sunny Saturday, after a birthday party, they were driving home. Suddenly, Tom started speeding and shifting lanes like he was driving in the Grand Prix. Alex kept asking Tom to slow down, further aggravating him, and he went even faster. She wanted to protect her daughter, who was in the back seat. So, Alex asked Tom to stop the car in the middle of the highway, believing he would drive safer without her in the car because his anger was seemingly all Alex's fault. Alex got out of the car to calm Tom's rage down. As Tom sped away, she prayed he would slow down now that she was out of the vehicle.

Aside from trying to keep the peace, active survivors also value their relationships. Women that score high in agreeableness prioritize their commitment and duty as mates, so they are willing to make sacrifices. The loyal, conscientious partner keeps trying to please her PL, hoping he will be satisfied and less cruel if she does what he wants a little better. Yet no matter how effective the survivor is in keeping the peace or how efficient she is in protecting her children, the chronic emotional pain and stress of enduring a traumatic bond inevitably create a slew of trauma symptoms in victims.

Trauma develops from events outside of our everyday experiences. Traumatic bonding is not merely dysfunctional; it is beyond the scope of a typical romance. Traumatic bonding causes 100 percent of women the distressing symptoms of loss of self and cognitive dissonance. And 25 to 50 percent develop C-PTSD.[4]

LOSS OF SELF

Traumatic bonding's two conditions—the power differential and intermittent abuse—are directly related to trauma symptoms. The PL's power in the trauma bond grows over time due to his threats, insults, and domination. A tragic outcome of living with a controlling, selfish PL is the survivor's diminishing sense of self. Losing oneself in a relationship is like peeling an onion—it happens gradually, one layer at a time, until nothing is left.

Do you recall purchasing peace by neglecting yourself? Or prioritizing your partner no matter the personal cost? Or maybe you gave away your boundaries just to keep things working? The high price of these actions is the loss of your individuality and freedom. Because the PL demands to control the relationship's psychological space, a TBR woman loses her ability to act on her values and make decisions independently; she must sacrifice her identity to keep the couple's identity.

Juno described how she felt like a sacrificial lamb: "I had no autonomy to follow my passion or live my desired life. We didn't do much of what I wanted to do. And I had no time to be myself. I just surrendered to Larry and didn't care anymore."

A dominant man asserts his power over his partner, forcing her to abandon authentic beliefs and feelings. Initially, the woman might fight back when the PL plows through her boundaries. However, she is no match for the PL's sadistic cruelty and psychological manipulation.

Emotionally exhausted from the abuse, the AS will deny the harm, become passive, and reframe the trauma bond to be not so bad.

While these coping strategies provide immediate relief, they chip away at an active survivor's agency. When a woman is in a healthy relationship, she has agency, which is the ability to control her life and influence her thoughts and behavior. With agency, a woman feels competent to handle various tasks and situations and can be psychologically stable yet flexible.[5] However, with the survivor habitually suppressing herself and being told how useless, incapable, or stupid she is, she forgets how to act and feels unsure about what step to take.

Alex shared how she lost her agency: "My daughter would hear Tom calling me names—whore, slut, or whatever—repeatedly. I didn't know how to remove my daughter from the harm of my relationship without involving Child Protective Services and risking losing her. I had to keep the peace and somehow make my daughter feel safe. I completely lost my ability to take appropriate action. I became a zombie." However, the psychological violence usually recurs and escalates despite the active survivor's efforts to appease the PL.

The PL's chronic, hostile mocking, sarcasm, and insults make his partner lose her self-esteem and feel insecure. The PL's lies make her question her perception of reality. When she confronts him, he gaslights her by minimizing the betrayal, claiming that nothing has happened and that she is overreacting. He constantly turns the tables on her, and his intentional manipulation lowers the survivor's confidence. Her self-doubt increases even in areas in which she previously demonstrated skill.[6] The AS believes she is incompetent. Keri explained, "I lost trust in my ability to reason. I often don't trust myself to make decisions or determine my next steps. I don't know who I am anymore. So, how can I trust myself? And all that eats away at my confidence. I'm trying to find my way in the dark."

COGNITIVE DISSONANCE:
AN INTERNAL MENTAL WAR

While enduring your trauma bond, how often do you ask yourself: "Do I love him or hate him? Is he my lover or torturer? Is this relationship toxic or nourishing?" I know these questions ping-pong in your brain and overwhelm you. That is because, due to the two sides of a PL's mask and intermittent abuse, the cognitive dissonance (CD) you initially felt deepens after you spend more time in your traumatic attachment. "CD is the paralyzing psychological reaction to being indecisively held in an exploitative relationship with someone whom you both love and hate."[7]

The dual sides of Jekyll/Hyde create confusion and a constant conflict in your mind. You have experiences of him love-bombing you and promising you the moon. And then betraying and intimidating you. Your CD is severe because it happens in three ways: about him, you, and the relationship. The two-sided persona of your PL causes your head to spin: "Is he my 'soulmate' or a 'soul slayer'?" Women swing between "I can't live without him" and "I can't live with him." He continually has two contradictory patterns; he is both caring and sadistic.[8]

In healthy relationships, people don't struggle with two very different representations of the same person. There is consistency in personality, word, and action. A TBR wages war on our perception of reality because how can contradictory feelings or beliefs be true?

CD also impacts how we think about ourselves. We feel best when our behaviors, thoughts, and feelings align with our values and beliefs. Yet, an attachment to a PL does not allow that to happen. For example, when you are forced to do something you don't want to do, conflict is created between your thoughts ("I didn't want to do this") and behavior ("I did it"). You must contradict yourself to keep your lover's adoration, like when Keri agreed to stay in her joyless research career to please Nick or when Juno tolerated Larry's insults and betrayal.

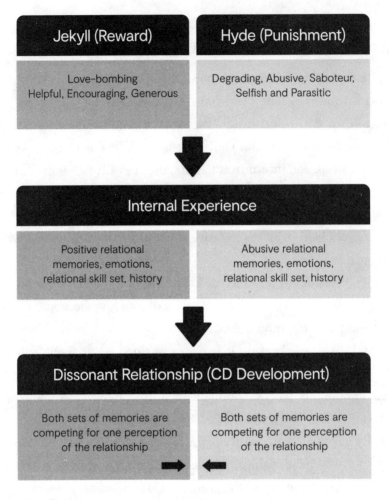

When you violate your values consistently, you can no longer recognize yourself. Gaslighting, manipulation, and intimidation erode your self-esteem. Because you forget how you once functioned, you live in constant brain fog. These injuries to self-perception significantly reduce thinking clearly.[9] It's no wonder you ask, "Is it me? Am I the crazy, cruel one?"

Lily hung her head in shame, recounting all the moments when she had behaved irrationally—throwing a drink in Jason's face when she caught him with another woman, installing nanny cams in his bedroom, creating fake accounts to catfish him, showing up unannounced, verbally lacerating him after each lie and betrayal. She tearfully recalled the moment her CD peaked: "Dr. Nae, I was standing in the bathroom in your office, and I looked at myself in the mirror while washing my hands. The person I saw looked like me, but at the same time, I couldn't recognize her. She looked so dead inside. I wondered if I was asleep and having a nightmare; it felt surreal. And the feeling of living in a dream state continued for many weeks." CD often induces a feeling of dissociation like the one Lily described.

An AS also experiences contradictory feelings about the relationship: "This is the happiest I have felt and the most broken." Your memories of a sweet beginning, incredible make-up sex, and luxurious vacations conflict with brutal memories of the silent treatment and lying right to your face about having sex with another woman. Consequently, the AS has as many positive perceptions of her relationship as traumatic ones. And the pleasant memories from the beginning of the relationship block the survivor's ability to realize her TBR's damaging effects fully. She asks herself, "Is it that bad? I must be exaggerating some of it. Am I making too much out of his controlling behaviors?" CD keeps her stuck.

According to Sandra L. Brown, MA, while in a TBR, the survivor's CD is "chronic and persistent."[10] The PL's personas and behaviors create her confusion, so she is forever exposed to the source of her trauma. Also, the duration of time spent in the TBR will affect the severity of the survivor's CD. All reasons why she stays stuck.

Research has shown that women who score high in agreeableness and conscientiousness are prone to develop CD. Her cooperative nature makes her tolerate the inconsistencies in her PL's behavior. And achievement-oriented women will do anything to make the relationship succeed. Also, they are guided by high-minded values, so will experience brutal confusion when they violate their principles and continue to stay in the relationship.[11]

CD creates the trauma symptoms of fear and helplessness due to her longing to stay with him even though he has hurt her many times. Or, as one of my patients said, "The illogical trauma bonded side of me makes me feel powerless to leave him." Combining the survivor's personality with the many layers of CD causes her to have a spaghetti brain. Over time, her capacity to plan, concentrate, and make rational decisions disappear. These mental processes are called executive functioning. And when your executive functioning system is compromised, your judgment and ability to think rationally go offline.

CD is a severe trauma symptom that confuses the survivor and causes the rational decision-making part of her brain to crash. It keeps her trapped because she is always comparing and trying to reconcile her conflicting emotions and competing experiences of her traumatic attachment.[12]

COMPLEX PTSD SYMPTOMS

As I mentioned in chapter four, C-PTSD is a set of trauma symptoms resulting from long-term exposure to abuse or neglect in childhood. C-PTSD is a relational version of post-traumatic stress disorder. The trauma symptoms are complex because they are caused by a chronic violation of power and trust between two emotionally connected people. Trauma bonds are a prime example of relational trauma due to the pathological lover controlling, manipulating, and abusing their lover. And unfortunately, over time, the extreme fear and stress that the survivor feels cause several, if not all, C-PTSD symptoms.

C-PTSD symptoms in the survivor can include

- a negative sense of self (or a loss of self, as I described earlier)
- difficulty controlling emotions, and
- distrust toward others.

The survivor might also experience some PTSD symptoms, such as

- a sense of feeling threatened,

- avoidance of the threat, and

- re-experiencing the threat through intrusive thoughts or feelings (flashbacks).

C-PTSD symptoms develop simultaneously and intensify as the trauma bond increases. Therefore, C-PTSD symptoms from a TBR make a woman feel like she has been at war, terrorized by an enemy. Hence, she needs emotional triage work to help her heal, which will be explained in the last section of the book. C-PTSD symptoms are a set of learned responses to chronic domination, betrayal, abuse, and manipulation. I have organized the symptoms into five categories: **intrusive, depressive, avoidant, relational**, and **physical**.[13] Let's take a look at each one.

Intrusive Symptoms: Overwhelming Emotions that Strike like Lightning

EMOTIONAL DISTRESS, ANXIETY, AND FEAR

Emotions help us give meaning to the experience of being alive. The butterflies in your stomach, lump in your throat, beating of your heart, and warmth in your face give you feedback about yourself and the world. Unfortunately, survivors frequently experience being overwhelmed by fear, anxiety, helplessness, and hypervigilance. The darker dimensions of love have caused these distressing feelings to override positive ones in the survivor.

The emotion that survivors express to me the most is fear—fear of what will become of them, fear of what they have lost or will lose, terror about what lies ahead, and an endless list of what-ifs. A PL's dominating and unpredictable behavior has caused the survivor to feel terrorized. The survivor's body has been and continues to live in a state of chronic fear and alarm.

Intrusive, unwanted thoughts which happen repeatedly are called *ruminations.* How will I survive this? Did my partner lie to me? How do I escape this madness? Obsessive thoughts are caused by a fixed switch in the brain that signals we are unsafe, creating overwhelming anxiety. Pondering those questions and not coming up with answers creates anxiety. Even worse, when you don't come up with an action-able plan and instead answer with "I can't do it," "It won't work out," or "I will never recover," you are scaring yourself. Scaring yourself by engaging in repetitive negative thoughts is distressing. You are scaring yourself when you tell yourself that the uncertainty you feel will last forever. Also, humans need control. And we think that by overthinking and worrying, we can be in control.

Insomnia is another common symptom, and it is caused by over-thinking. It may be harder to fall asleep or stay asleep; some survivors wake up often at night and can't fall back asleep due to rumination. As a result, survivors struggle to get restorative or restful sleep, creating anxiety, depression, irritability, and other symptoms.

When a survivor has lived in a chronic state of fear, her nervous system becomes accustomed to being on high alert for threats and con-tinues to do so even once she is safe. Big, negative emotions such as anxiety, fear, anger, rage, and hypervigilance are intrusive and make it difficult for a survivor to concentrate or be present because she feels like she is still living in the trauma vortex.

ANGER AND RAGE

Survivors have to repress a lot of anger to survive a trauma bond. Therefore, these women swim in a reservoir of resentment over their partner's exploitation of their love and betrayal of their trust. Sweeping emotions of anger and rage that follow years of injustice hijack the women. Emotional hijacking refers to how strong emotions, such as fear or anger, can overpower your thoughts and behaviors.[14]

Many women come into my office session after session with their heads hung in shame and disappointment as they described how they lost it on their children or got into a raging fight with their friends. Experiencing road rage, impatience, or feeling like you're one minor move away from ripping someone's head off are all symptoms of repressed anger and rage breaking through the surface. Emotions do not go away just because we don't feel them—the energy must come up and out somehow.

The repression of anger over time can also cause anxiety.[15] Also, some women turn their rage inward, which leads to depression or even suicidal thoughts. Juno, at one point, said she felt so depressed that she was crying in the corner and stating, "I don't want to be on this earth anymore." Instead of soothing her, Larry decided to record her and say to her, "See, I told you—you're the sick one!" Many women who have left trauma bonds must work to get in touch with their righteous anger, which requires learning to speak up, be assertive, and express anger. And some need to work on managing or calming their anger down.

HYPERVIGILANCE: LIVING ON HIGH ALERT

Women who have suffered from chronic, repeated abuse at their lover's hands have spent periods feeling anxious or panicked, so their nervous system is hyperaroused and hypervigilant. And women who have been lied to repeatedly about cheating are hyper-suspicious. Hypervigilance means you are constantly on guard or highly sensitive to your surroundings; the brain does this automatically to ensure your safety.[16] Hypervigilance feels like having a pair of eyes on the front, back, and sides of your head. The survivor's nervous system is on permanent alert and never feels secure. If you are hypervigilant, you always look for hidden dangers or secrets. The survivor scans a room within seconds. She reads energy and body language, listens for unspoken messages, pieces things together (whether they go together or not), startles easily, and can be highly sensitive to sound. Hypervigilance can leave you exhausted and anxious.

EXTREME STARTLE REFLEX

Another common symptom I've witnessed in survivors is an extreme startle reflex. Without a history of trauma, the startle reflex is intended to jump-start the body in the case of emergencies. We stop, pause, brace, tighten our muscles, hold our breath, investigate, and respond by either waiting out the danger or acting. Then the body returns to a normal state. If the threat is severe or constant, the startle pattern deepens and becomes a stress response.[17] Many women who have left their PLs feel startled if they get texts or emails from them or hear their ex-lover's name mentioned; some women even start shaking. This startle reflex is caused by years of intimidation and feeling threatened by their PLs.

FLASHBACKS: A WAKING NIGHTMARE

A flashback is much more than a memory—it involves feeling the same feelings and sensations experienced during the trauma. Emotional flashbacks are perhaps the most common and viscerally felt C-PTSD symptoms.[18] Even when the survivor is not in the presence of the PL's intimidation or cruelty, the survivor's body re-experiences the event.

Renowned therapist and author Lori Gottlieb famously coined the phrase, "If it's hysterical, it's historical," meaning that if our reaction in the present moment is out of proportion to whatever triggered our response, the trigger is based on something in the past.[19] Historical threats cause psychological distress, which manifests as physical symptoms.

For example, Keri spoke about how hard it was to deal with the failure of her marriage after trying so hard. She said there were times that she felt overwhelmed by uncomfortable feelings in her body; she would have panic attacks "out of nowhere." One day she was grocery shopping and a man looked at her the way Nick used to. She left her full grocery cart in the aisle, ran out of the store, and drove home hyperventilating. Her hysterical reaction was historical in nature.

Depressive Symptoms: Emotions that Feel like Rock Bottom

SHAME, BLAME, HOPELESSNESS

If hypervigilance is on one end of the spectrum of C-PTSD symptoms, hypo (low) vigilance is on the other side. The main depressive symptoms of C-PTSD are shame, hopelessness, and despair.[20] For survivors, depression may be experienced as a feeling of "I can't" due to feeling trapped and powerless.

Shame is the primary cause of misery for many women in a trauma bond even after they leave. Shame causes us to overthink our deficiencies relentlessly, focus on our flaws, believe we are unworthy of love, and that our future is hopeless. Juno sobbed deeply, "I'm an utter failure. Love never works out for me because I'm unlovable; it's my fault. And the worst part is that nothing is ever going to change." What a grim perspective to live in; shame is a soul murderer. Survivors are ashamed of staying, enduring, causing, and leaving. They live in the impossible dynamic of "damned if I do, damned if I don't." You name it, and the survivor will find something to feel ashamed about.

A PL doesn't necessarily blame you for every event—they might even sometimes apologize or fake remorse. Still, their overall manipulation pattern always includes repeated efforts to make you feel you are the cause of the abuse.[21] One of my patients described how she experienced three levels of blame. First, her husband blames her, then she blames herself, and then she blames herself for blaming herself.

Shame and self-blame are unbearable because they are unrelenting voices that tell us we have failed as human beings, there is nothing we can do to change it, and since we cannot change it, we are a failure. Shame and self-blame perpetuate hopelessness.

Juno repeatedly expressed that she hates herself for falling for Larry, tolerating his abuse and cheating, and then being stupid enough for him to put her in jail. "I promised myself I would protect myself even when I fell in love, and I did the absolute opposite."

Avoidance Symptoms: Putting a Band-Aid on a Bullet Wound

SUBSTANCE USE, NUMBING BEHAVIORS, AND SHAME-SPIRAL

A typical behavioral response to traumatic bonding is avoidance. Avoidance involves learned patterns of shutting out or pushing away uncomfortable sensations, memories, or emotions. We want to avoid any situation that reminds us of the fear and terror we endured. Sometimes this involves avoiding situations, people, and places that are reminders of the past toxic relationship.[22] To a certain extent, avoidance can initially help keep us safe, but it quickly interferes with our progress and healing.

Avoidance behaviors, such as excessive binge-watching, procrastinating, and mindlessly scrolling through social media, are great distractions from feeling shame, anger, and anxiety. Putting off answering calls, texts, or emails from your divorce attorney due to feeling ashamed and incompetent is a normal response to a violent attachment. However, avoidance drives overthinking, and overthinking creates anxiety. Once anxiety takes over, instead of acting, you keep avoiding life and staying stuck, perpetuating the experience of being trauma bonded.

To be trapped in a TBR is to be in intolerable pain and can cause you to lean on unhealthy coping mechanisms to avoid feeling altogether. Also, living with a controlling and abusive lover can push you toward addictive habits. Emotional eating, drinking, or drugs may be relied upon to soothe your suffering and loneliness and fill the emotional holes caused by IPV. You need something outside yourself to remove the terrible feelings inside; you need a mood-altering experience. Drugs and alcohol help to numb the pain of intentional betrayal and coercive control. Yet, they can quickly become an addiction, even without having an "addictive personality" or a family history of addiction. Substance addiction can happen with enough use, as you need certain chemical levels to soothe your pain and shame.

Living in a TBR can make a survivor especially vulnerable to addiction because addictions stem from a brain's reward system dysfunction. The survivor feels so bad that she needs strong hits of dopamine, the "feel good" neurotransmitter, to compensate for her loneliness, anxiety, fear, and anger. The only way that Juno could deal with Larry's unfaithfulness was to drink a bottle of chardonnay every night and pop Xanax. Her blood work showed liver damage when she visited the doctor for a general checkup.

Addictions fuel a shame spiral—she feels shame about her trauma bond and numbs herself with substances. She feels shame about needing substances to soothe the pain. She hides her coping mechanisms or calms herself with other self-harming actions. Her addictive actions and hiding create self-hatred, which feeds her shame more, and round and round she goes.

Finally, avoidance may blind you from seeing your PL for the monster he is. You might still focus on his positive traits rather than accept how damaging the relationship was. Remember the sentimental spiral from earlier? Sometimes Alex would repeat the same sentiment, "If only I could have loved him better, he wouldn't have been so mean to me." Due to the cognitive dissonance mentioned earlier, active survivors continue to avoid the brutal truth about their PL.

Relational Symptoms: Connection Cutoffs

INABILITY TO TRUST, SELF-ISOLATION, AND INNER CRITIC

Of course, a TBR survivor will be afraid to trust again. She has learned that trusting someone consistently leads to pain, so why would she ever believe anyone again? When you have been tortured in a TBR, it is customary to generalize your experience—survivors feel that no one can be trusted.

A trauma bond experience is so disconcerting and undermines our sense of self in such totality that you may feel like an alien on a foreign planet. Trauma bonds are life-altering experiences because we will never be the same person as before. This is not to say that we are better off or worse; we are simply different (and with time and healing, hopefully, eventually better). But if it takes an entire book, hundreds of researchers, and several decades of studies to capture the experience of enduring and recovering from a trauma bond, how does one explain that experience to a friend, coworker, acquaintance, family member, or the average therapist? It feels like an impossible task, and TBR survivors do not have the time and energy for another impossible task. Thus, you may feel burdened by relationships and resort to self-isolating. A key component of relationships is relating to others, yet how can those fortunate to have never experienced a TBR relate to how a survivor's mind-body feels and operates?

A TBR leaves you questioning every element of who you are, which makes it especially difficult to maintain or form friendships. It is a terrifying experience to let others in. It is not uncommon for survivors to terminate certain friendships or relationships during a TBR. Hence why survivors feel so isolated.

Many women develop a harsh inner critic from a trauma bond. This inner critic causes them to defensively avoid others for fear that they will judge and criticize them too. Defensively avoiding others drives her to believe the inner critic in her head because she does not have experiences that prove it wrong, experiences in which people are accepting and respectful of her.

Physical Symptoms: System Failure
COMPROMISED IMMUNE SYSTEM AND CHRONIC ILLNESS

Finally, traumatic bonding significantly affects the survivor's physical health. When stressful situations persist, the body remains highly alert without the ability to rest. The body will continue to produce high amounts of stress chemicals (such as cortisol) when stress is ongoing. However, C-PTSD is associated with chronically low cortisol levels within the bloodstream. This does not mean that your body is producing less cortisol. In fact, the body continues to release high amounts of stress chemicals. In cases of chronic stress, your body changes how it processes cortisol.

As a result, C-PTSD is associated with frequent bursts of high and low cortisol symptoms. Chronic stress caused by traumatic bonding affects the survivor's immune system. When bloodstream cortisol levels are high, the immune system is suppressed. In contrast, the immune system thrives when bloodstream cortisol levels are low. In more simplistic terms, stress weakens immune system functioning.

The immune system is associated with inflammation in the body. This inflammation is necessary for fighting off a virus. However, when the immune system continues to inflame without a target, there is a greater likelihood of long-term physical health problems. Keri described many powerful sensations in her body throughout her twenty-year marriage to Nick and even after. She had chronic tightness in her stomach and had been diagnosed with irritable bowel syndrome and relenting back pain. Decades of research from Bessel van der Kolk and others have documented a clear, direct, and irrefutable connection between prolonged trauma (stress) and physical ailments and illness.[23]

Thus, traumatic bonding dramatically affects physical and mental health. Health problems associated with chronic stress caused by traumatic bonding include high blood pressure, food cravings, addictions, sluggish digestion, suppressed immunity, sleep disturbances, and autoimmune disorders. Do you experience any of these physical symptoms?

This chapter allows you to deepen your understanding of the trauma symptoms caused by TBRs. And because all survivors have cognitive dissonance, and some have C-PTSD, many are doubly traumatized. Also, I know this list is long and can be hard to read. Yet I hope it allows you to put into words what you have been feeling and experiencing. Unfortunately, women all over the world endure this encounter and develop their set of symptoms from traumatic bonding. Here's the good news: you are not alone, and now we have words for what you have endured. The emotional part of our brain (called the limbic system) loves categories. As my favorite psychiatrist, Dan Siegal, says, "We must name it to tame it."[24] I, along with my patients and many others, know it is possible to recover from traumatic bonding. And in the last section of the book, I offer tools and skills you can use to support your recovery from traumatic bonding.

KEY POINTS TO REMEMBER

1. Traumatic bonding's two foundational conditions—the power differential and intermittent abuse—are directly related to your trauma symptoms. Traumatic bonding causes distressing symptoms of **loss of self, cognitive dissonance, and complex post-traumatic stress disorder (C-PTSD).**

2. **Loss of Self:** A trauma-bonded woman purchases peace by neglecting herself, prioritizing her partner, and giving away her boundaries. She must sacrifice her identity to keep the couple's identity. The PL's maltreatment makes her insecure, which causes her to develop an unstable self-image. His lies make her question her perception of reality. His gaslighting and manipulation lower her confidence, and her self-doubt increases even in areas in which she previously demonstrated skill until she finally believes she is incompetent.

3. **Cognitive Dissonance (CD):** a mental state in which one feels extreme discomfort due to holding two conflicting beliefs or doing something that goes against your values. CD is a severe symptom, which causes a survivor to ping-pong

between the two realities of how she perceives her lover, herself, and the relationship.

4. **C-PTSD** is a condition where you experience some symptoms of PTSD along with additional signs of a **negative sense of self, difficulty controlling your emotions, and distrust toward others.**

5. **C-PTSD** symptoms are a set of learned responses to chronic domination and manipulation. Symptoms are organized into five categories:

   a. **Intrusive symptoms:** emotional distress, anxiety, fear, anger, rage, hypervigilance, flashbacks

   b. **Depressive symptoms:** shame, blame, hopelessness

   c. **Avoidance** symptoms: substance use, numbing behaviors, shame spiral

   d. **Relational symptoms:** inability to trust, self-isolation, inner critic

   e. **Physical symptoms**: compromised immune system, chronic illness

6

Getting off the Merry-Go-Round of Insanity

The most beautiful people we have known are those
who have known defeat, suffering, struggle, loss, and
have found their way out of the depth.[1]

—ELISABETH KUBLER-ROSS

THE CONDITIONS OF INTERMITTENT ABUSE and power imbalance allow a traumatic attachment to develop, and CD keeps you bonded. Therefore, the dynamics of a TBR are complex. Hence leaving this pathological attachment is challenging. Yet, never leaving is much more tragic. Parting comes with risks, so staying can feel like the lesser of two evils. A survivor's self-doubt, fear, and confusion keep her trapped and controlled. TBR survivors who wish for the control, manipulation, and emotional abuse to stop are usually disappointed to learn firsthand that it never does. The only thing that stops abuse is leaving.

Through my clinical practice, I have observed common themes of why women leave. Many women have an epiphany and realize they are not physically, emotionally, or financially safe. Some survivors emotionally detach over time and leave once they feel sufficiently numb. Others get a self-esteem boost outside the home through education, work, or community and realize they genuinely don't need their PL. The general theme is that survivors get to a point where the pain of staying is worse than the fear of leaving.

No matter the reason for leaving, escaping a TBR is dangerous, as there is no way to predict how it will unfold. Ninety percent of coercive control victims report experiencing post-separation abuse (PSA).[2] Post-separation abuse often harms domestic abuse victims for years or decades after separation. In some cases, the violence continued and even worsened. However, I've also seen cases where survivors were terrified, and we prepared for the worst-case scenario, yet walking out did not lead to continued abuse.

There is always a last-straw incident. Unfortunately, this straw comes after years of coercive control and dominance, and the damage is profound.[3] This chapter explains the numerous breaking points that push women to go. Research shows that for some women, the most dangerous time is when a TBR ends. So, this chapter also explains how to exit a TBR safely. Here's the reality of a TBR exodus—it was not a ten-day walk into the relationship, and it won't be a ten-day walk out.

BREAKING POINTS: SYMPTOMS OF LIBERATION

Pathological lovers steal everything in the woman's personality that could serve his needs. The PL is a selfish lover because he equates love to being "serviced," like a car in a garage, a massage client, or a restaurant customer. The PL has bottomless needs and a vampiristic heart. Hence, one day his lover has an aha moment: he is incapable of truly loving her.

Though the survivor is determined to leave, she has fears. Can I survive on my own? What will the economic consequence be? How will fleeing impact my children? Will my PL destroy me if I go? Can

I survive his retaliation? The PL's previous threats fuel her fear: "If you leave, I will hunt you down and make your life a living hell." Or, as Jordan said to me, "The only way you're leaving this marriage is in a body bag." These threats create the belief that your PL will react violently once you begin the process of leaving.

On average, trauma-bonded women make four to seven attempts before finally escaping.[4] Lily tried six times before finally breaking free. Keri contemplated leaving for several years. Juno kicked Larry out numerous times, but he always won her over and returned.

A victim's loss of self and lack of safety means she must detach or die. A pathological lover will use you and your resources until you have an empty heart, an empty bank account, and a dried-up soul. Hear me when I say this: patience and support do not work with a pathological partner, and second chances quickly turn into tenth chances. And don't even think about trying "tough love" since it involves a responsibility to educate an abusive partner who has no interest in learning (despite his saying otherwise). In a TBR, the wisest, safest, and most effective thing is to make yourself unavailable, disengage, and escape.

Losing Yourself

PLs are masters at using intermittent abuse and unpredictable emotional connection to have power and control over their partners. Survivors were forced to disown their needs and desires to maintain peace. They denied the hostile abuse and remained passive to stay bonded to their PL—because they value relationships. Survivors purchased affection by giving away their boundaries, allowing the PLs to dominate. To avoid conflict, survivors abandoned themselves. Loving a PL meant disconnecting from their authentic self and personal power. Survivors leave when their sense of self has been destroyed to the point that they no longer recognize themselves.

A survivor's loss of self affects their functioning, even in areas that do not relate to their love life. For example, Keri, a prolific researcher, doubted her ability to make work decisions. Juno, who had years of sobriety under her belt, lost her self-respect when she began drinking again. Alex, confident and self-assured, lost her ability to trust herself. Lily, who had worked hard to get into her dream school, sacrificed her college experience and almost gave up her dream of being a therapist. Each survivor slowly woke up and decided they would not let themselves get erased by their relationship. This evoked the desire to reclaim themselves.

Losing Your Joy

Vivacious, outgoing women look and feel like a shell of a human toward the end of their TBR. Patients report a loss of enjoyment as a wake-up call. This loss is accompanied by feelings of emptiness, lack of freedom, hopelessness, anxiety, depression, and worthlessness, often culminating in suicidal thoughts. Juno explained her experience this way:

> I felt horrible, but I was too depressed to do anything about it. I was getting sick from being so stressed out all the time, which made me more depressed. My mental health was gone. I didn't want to die, but I wished for death because at least that would make my misery disappear. I had suicidal thoughts all the time. I felt hopeless, anxious, depressed, and trapped. I tried to kick Larry out and failed every time, destroying my self-worth.

Losing Your Health

Most survivors report that the breakdown in their health and daily functioning woke them up because life with a PL is intolerable. The PL doesn't care that his partner is sick, fatigued, or anxious. His needs still get met, and God forbid he takes care of his ailing partner. Many patients experience extreme stress levels and sleep disturbances, like Alex:

> My body was so stressed and fatigued. I could feel my immune system getting weaker by the minute, and I was getting sick constantly. On top of that, I was so emotionally strung out that I would fluctuate between feeling anxious and being a zombie. I just wanted to sleep, but when I lay down, I was wide awake. Being alive felt like a chore. My body shouted at me, trying to tell me that this toxic relationship was poisoning my body, mind, and soul.

The PL cannot understand that love implies a moral obligation to care for his lover's well-being. One of my patients, Kelly, explained that for years, she had put up with her husband Derek's emotional abuse, coercive control, and drug addiction. She had tried everything to save her marriage. Kelly described to me the drastic scene that was her turning point.

They had gone to a drug counselor due to Derek's severe cocaine addiction. They booked another appointment with the therapist for the next day, yet only Kelly showed up. The therapist said, "Kelly, if you don't leave Derek, you will get cancer." The drug counselor's words stung her like no other advice or lecture about Derek's drug addiction had. "Your husband is a severe drug addict, and you are enabling him. I believe the toxicity in your daily relationship is physically weakening your immune system. Derek did not join you here today for our second session. He has no intention of getting sober. He needs a dramatic intervention, or his behaviors will continue to poison you and your child." The counselor's piercing words snapped Kelly out of her TBR coma.

Feeling Unsafe

One of my patients, Lisa, was married to a very wealthy diplomat. He was in federal criminal court due to money laundering. During the initial court proceedings, she'd decided to "stand by her man." One evening after court Lisa couldn't calm her nerves, so her husband gave her two tranquilizers, which made her very dizzy. She fell, hit her head, and blacked out. Luckily, she did not end up with a traumatic brain injury, yet the drugs and fall crystallized how her physical safety was endangered by staying with him.

Fearing for Your Children

Keri finally realized that her life was of no value to Nick. Her only value was the money and free labor she brought to the relationship. She reached a turning point after Nick threw their daughter Stella in the trunk of their car. She decided it was time to get away from the madness. Often women can do for their children what they can't do for themselves. Keri knew she had to protect her daughters from Nick's rage.

Lily's parents were in a trauma-bonded marriage for over twenty years, and naturally, Lily and her sister became trauma bonded to their dad, who was extremely toxic. There were endless signs of abuse, yet Lily's mother, a hard-working immigrant, could never work up the courage to leave. It wasn't until Lily's sister came forward about being sexually abused by their dad that Lily's mom was able to escape. And even then, she struggled with believing the reality of whom she had married.

Feeling like an Emotional Hostage

Survivors start fantasizing about what life might be like if they didn't have a boot on their neck 24/7. What could it be like waking up in a safe home? What would it be like to fall asleep without anxiety, wondering where he is? Over time, survivors edge toward being done feeling like emotional hostages. Survivors only have so much tolerance for being coercively controlled and abused. So, like trapped prisoners, you start thinking about breaking free. Survivor stories amplify how their trauma bond experiences depleted their ability to have agency. Alex explained, "How did I transform from someone who was confident and seemed to have her life together to feeling completely incapable of making my own decisions and living my own life?"

Finding Confidence Elsewhere

PLs attack their partners daily, which leaves them questioning their abilities and worth. Survivors who are highly conscientious hold on tightly to anything that gives them a sense of achievement because that is their lifeline. A survivor will often begin growing their sense of confidence in other areas. They might turn to friends, their career, family, or other sources to bolster their self-esteem. It takes a trifecta of affirming sources to override the PLs abuse, to nudge the survivor to go.

The night Lily discovered Jason's double life, she left him sleeping in her apartment while she walked outside and called a friend. With her friend's support, they processed what she had just learned. Her friend reassured her she was strong enough to walk away for good. Lily's decision to end it was reinforced by the confidence she gained from her work. The pandemic had just begun, and she was an essential worker thriving in her job. In her eyes, Jason was a cheating, drug-addicted loser. With all her ducks in a row, she got out.

Devalued and Discarded

Some controlling men take the initiative to end the relationship. They do this to maintain control and protect their fragile egos; "better to dump than be dumped" is their motto. Your lover was the sun, the moon, the north star, and the cosmos. As their final act, they deal you another devastating blow when they channel their inner Ariana Grande and say, "Thank you, next!" You were a trophy when you were meeting his needs for power, money, status, and pleasure. Yet, despite how good it may feel, treating someone as a trophy means you are being objectified, quite literally. A PL's display of interest in his trophy partner has little to do with love; his partner is a sparkly toy that he owns and shows off to the admiring crowd.

The PL cannot comprehend that love can only exist between two equals: two subjects—not two objects. Love cannot be put in a contract, bought, controlled, or taken by force. Yet, his partner is an object, so after her usefulness diminishes, he discards her. The PL has paved the groundwork for months before his exit, yet his partner might not have recognized the signs. The abuser may hint over time that D-day is coming, or the moment could arrive suddenly and be unexpected.

PL men often end the relationship selfishly and cruelly. They leave because their never-ending thirst for new supplies is insatiable. He has found another woman who is younger, more affluent, obedient, or desirable. Or maybe he wants to pursue his fantasy of his dream woman who does everything for him and never challenges him. Indeed, these decisions are reflections of the PL's sadistic selfishness.

Many controlling men will do everything they can to hurt their partners on their way out the door: blaming her, stealing her money or other possessions, or smearing her name. Also, some PLs crave retaliation for how they feel you hurt them. Which includes the times you defended yourself, questioned the superiority of his knowledge, and refused to be a carbon copy of him. Being rejected can leave a woman feeling worthless and even suicidal.

Larry knew he was going to leave Juno for his new lover. Yet instead of telling her, he blamed her for his affair. Larry's cheating crushed Juno, and she turned to drugs and alcohol. She was no use to him once he had a better, more enticing offer. Juno and Larry never processed their relationship after he put Juno in jail. PLs do not possess the ability to communicate, and indeed, ending a ten-year relationship requires some communication. PLs do not do humane endings because they are not humane people.

KEY POINTS TO REMEMBER

1. Women leave trauma bonds due to a lack of physical, emotional, and financial safety. There is always a last-straw incident, but the general theme is that survivors get to a point where they are more afraid to stay than to leave. The precise time to go is the survivor's decision alone, yet on average, trauma-bonded women make four to seven attempts before finally escaping.

2. Several factors contribute to a woman's decision to finally leave:

   - Chronic self-abandonment, which leads to a breakdown in functioning in other areas of life.

   - Loss of enjoyment of life, which induces severe depression, anxiety, and hopelessness.

   - Loss of physical health, which leaves her feeling weak, fatigued, and constantly sick.

   - Loss of safety, which wakes her up to the fear she feels every day.

   - Fearing for the safety of her children, which bypasses her low self-worth by motivating her to care for other vulnerable individuals.

   - She feels like an emotional hostage, which leads her to fantasize about what life would be like if she were free.

   - She feels confident in other areas of life, which gives her confidence to stand on her own two feet.

   - Being devalued and discarded (dumped) by the pathological lover.

7 | How to Leave Safely

> There is no safe way to remain in a relationship with a person
> who has no conscience. The only solution is to escape.
>
> **—DR. NAE**

THE EXACT PROCESS OF TELLING your partner the relationship is
over and collecting your stuff or getting him to move out can be com-
plicated and dangerous. When an abuser feels he's losing control, it is
often the most treacherous time for a survivor.[1] Telling a PL that it's
over is the equivalent of dropping a bomb on him. So, when you say
those words, he hears that it's time for war—and he will not hold back.
The PL will attack you from ALL sides, so it's crucial to be strategic
and have all your bases covered. He will ruthlessly lie as you've never
seen before. He will fabricate ridiculous stories and paint himself out
to be the victim. He will do everything to bait you into acting like a
"crazy bitch" to support his victim narrative. If you fall for the bait, the
consequences could be high, like ending up on a psychiatric hold or
in jail because of a restraining order against you, as we saw with Juno.

He will call *everything* into question, including your ability to
care for your children. He will try to sever your access to children,

property, and finances. Unfortunately, setting up the survivor to make her look like the perpetrator is very common, and this is the stage at which most women come to me. He will try to divide and conquer if you have mutual friends, bringing people (sometimes including your own family) onto his team. He'll try to attack your public image and damage your reputation, credibility, or career. And if he has anything to hang over your head (pictures, videos, emails, texts, etc.), you better believe he'll use it as blackmail. So, how do you best avoid the worst of these reactions?

SAFE WAYS TO LEAVE

It is essential for you, as the survivor, to refrain from telling him you're leaving. You must be ten steps ahead of the PL to protect yourself emotionally, physically, socially, and financially.

Never Let Them See You Coming

Alex acted quietly, with initiative and determination. She pulled herself out of her feelings of despair, devised an ingenious plan to fool Tom, and acted incredibly submissive for some time to disarm him. And then, when he least expected it, she got a restraining order and kicked him out.

Often, a woman tries to get the controlling man to move out and leave her alone, but the PL hangs on like an angry, territorial pit bull. If you fear your partner, do not tell *him* to go, and never tell him you're leaving while you are alone with him. Ensure someone's nearby who could protect you or do it in a public setting—only once you have strategized. Whether you fear physical, financial, or emotional danger, developing a strategic plan will help you avoid even more trauma once the relationship ends and, most importantly, keep you safe.

All attempts to escape from a TBR are risky. No matter how detailed the plan is to ensure success, no matter how much support or expert advice, no one can predict how a person with a volatile personality and history of abuse will react. Be aware that some well-intentioned friends and family might try to persuade you to leave despite your judgment; it is not the time. Trust yourself. It is your life, and you are the only one to deal with the consequences. The precise time to leave is the survivor's decision alone.

Prepare for Violence

Suppose you are the center of your partner's life; he is likely to commit desperate acts of emotional or physical violence to keep his world from falling apart. Suppose he threatens to kill or physically harm you. You *must* call the police *immediately*. Do not take his threats as empty. The threat of abandonment will drive a pathological person to do extreme things. Alex knew she wanted to leave her husband but did not know how or when. We devised a plan: she would inform one friend that she was getting ready to go, and if her husband got violent, she was to text her friend to call the police and alert them. Sure enough, her husband got physical, Alex texted her friend, and the police came fifteen minutes later. Ten minutes later, Tom was in handcuffs, and she got an emergency temporary restraining order against him.

A patient of mine met with a divorce attorney weeks before she was ready to leave. This survivor explained the abuse she had endured while raising three children. She had two last straws. The first one included her husband trying to block her from getting life-saving surgery. He yelled at her doctors, "What do you know? My wife does not need surgery." And the second one was when he threw a wine bottle and glass at her after a Labor Day party at their house. The lawyer applied for an order of protection from the court, citing those abusive incidents and a few others that demonstrated he was a clear and present danger to her. She took the kids to school, and her husband got served with a restraining order as he left the house for work. With him out of the house and unable to return, she was safe to start the divorce proceedings officially.

Another one of my patients, Liz, had a turning point when her husband showed up at her daughter's kindergarten graduation drunk. During the ceremony, he loudly complained the whole time. Her husband wanted to do a collaborative divorce, so he hired a mediator. Yet halfway through their proceedings, the mediator told her, "I would not mediate with this person. He's insane." So, Liz got an attorney, filed for divorce, and was nice enough to call her husband and tell him he would be served. As she explained, "The devil's wrath came through the phone." So, she hung up. Luckily, Liz had documented through video and audio her years of abuse. This digital proof got her a restraining order for eighteen months.

Tell Him when He's Sober

Never tell an intoxicated partner you are leaving. They are the most dangerous when under the influence of alcohol or drugs because their impulsivity is uninhibited. Intoxicated PLs are extremely dangerous once you tell them you are leaving. When I told Jordan I was going, he threw all my clothes and jewelry into the fireplace, kicked me down the stairs, and drove my daughter and me into a garage door. I did not know he was high on cocaine at the time. If you tell a PL that you are leaving him when he is high, you are putting yourself and your children (if you have them) in unnecessary danger.

If your PL is depressed or has threatened or attempted suicide, he has low regard for human life—his and yours. Many become enraged and believe that if they can't have you, no one else can. Suicidal PLs are prone to becoming very violent toward survivors, increasing the risk for instances of homicide or murder-suicide. Research from the Centers for Disease Control and Prevention (CDC) shows that one in five homicide victims is killed by their lover.[2] Take any suicide or death threat seriously and do everything to protect yourself (and your children) from your PL. Informing a violent lover that you want to go increases your risk of severe physical injury. For PLs, getting what they want is a way of life. They are not hampered by guilt or remorse and thus do not have the inhibitions most people do.

Be Extra Careful if There's a History of Sexual Violence

If your TBR included rape or other forms of sexual assault, be very careful about telling your partner you are leaving while still living with him. Rape is not only violent, it is sadistic, and there's no telling how much *more* sadistic your lover will become once he knows you're exiting. Sexual violence suggests you are little more than a toy to be used when needed and discarded once you are no longer required. Telling him you are leaving can incite him to sexually harm and use you until you go.

Seek Legal Counsel and Document Everything

This brings me to my next topic: when leaving a TBR, you often will be in contact with a legal official. As I highlighted above, leaving may include seeking a restraining order or aid in filing for divorce. To escape safely, you should first seek consultation from trained legal professionals about certain aspects of the law, such as the difference between civil (obtaining an order of protection) and criminal actions (mandatory arrest). If leaving involves contact with legal officials (such as in divorce or other court proceedings), you would be wise also to have a high-conflict divorce coach who will help you strategize so you do not act out and appear to be the crazy one. A divorce coach can also teach you how to effectively document his abusive actions in such a way that it can be used in civil and criminal legal proceedings.

Prepare Your Finances and Documents

If you are financially dependent on your PL, you must stockpile money, financial statements, and essential documents secretly. You can consult with a banker, accountant, and divorce attorney to ensure you have all your ducks in a row. Make copies of absolutely everything and store them with a friend. Open your own credit cards and bank account, but ensure you have all your mail sent to a friend's place. Assemble a list of passwords to essential accounts and prepare to change all of them as soon as you leave (or hours before). If you plan on living somewhere else, contact the post office to have all your mail forwarded to the new address at least ten days ahead of leaving.

Begin filling a "go bag" that has a change of clothes, cash, some credit cards, gift cards, things for the children, prescriptions, medicine, critical legal documents, bank statements, credit card statements, social security cards, birth certificates, passports, and all the essential documents you would need should you have to run out in a hurry. Store that bag at a friend's house or at your place of employment, somewhere he will never find it. Make sure to take all your valuables with you, such as jewelry and designer items, as you can sell these through a pawn shop or a service such as The RealReal if you are strapped for cash.

Trust me, once you announce your intention to leave, all your access to your/his money will be cut off. Assets will be moved, bank accounts will be closed, and credit cards will be canceled. Here's a fact—he wasn't friendly to you when you were there for him, so imagine what he will be like once he views you as enemy number one.

Finally, if it is possible to access his phone, computer, or other devices safely, go through and delete any content that leaves you vulnerable: photos (be sure also to empty the "recently deleted" folders, sent folder, and trash), texts, cloud drives (such as Google Drive, Dropbox, or iCloud; again make sure to empty the trash folder), and anything else you can think of. As you go through, take pictures, or obtain copies of anything that incriminates him—this is useful in legal proceedings. You must be detailed and highly meticulous with this step to ensure you have covered all your bases and left zero evidence of being there.

Jason was not the first guy to betray Lily; she had been exploited and blackmailed by another pathological personality before. So, on the night she discovered Jason's double life, Lily had the foresight to delete absolutely everything from his phone quickly: all photos of her and them, all texts, all emails, any image of her on his social media accounts—she completely deleted herself out of his life and blocked him on all fronts before waking him up and confronting him. Doing so helped her stick to her decision for good and made their breakup as clean and easy as possible, which brings me to my next point.

WHAT HAPPENS AFTER YOU LEAVE?

Once you decide to leave, you will feel both relief and fear. No matter how hard you fought your PL while trauma bonded, you inevitably accommodated him. By leaving, you are no longer doing what the PL wants or demands. So, know that disobeying him may feel scary and threatening. Even though your PL caused you pain and fear, he was also the one to relieve your pain. But now you must feel the fear and soothe yourself. While this might feel like an impossible task, you are more than capable of doing it—you have survived a trauma bond, which is evidence of your indomitable spirit.

Be Aware of the Threat of Stalking

Even after their partners make it clear that the relationship is over, many men continue to engage in controlling and intimidating behaviors. If these efforts for contact are one-sided, this is called persistent pursuit—a form of stalking. Persistent pursuit can be terrifying. You've finally mustered the courage to leave your TBR, only to be further scared and harassed. But knowing the possibilities of how your PL will react can help you prepare to better get through this difficult time.

Usually, PLs who stalk do so in multiple ways. He might initiate contact, spread rumors, follow you, send inappropriate messages, break into your home, move into your neighborhood, cyberstalk you, or call you multiple times a day. Many of these behaviors are considered criminal harassment or other crimes. Be sure to document any actions of persistent pursuit, as this is grounds for a restraining order.

If your partner has access to guns, you are at an increased risk, even if he has never used them against you. If you file a restraining order, federal and state statutes usually prohibit people from legally possessing a gun once the order of protection has been granted.

DARVO

Get ready for DARVO. After leaving a trauma bond, your pathological lover will use the deny, attack, and reverse victim and offender (DARVO) tactic to manipulate and control you continually. The PL will shift the focus away from their abuse and coercive control by making false allegations against you. The PL intends to switch the roles of victim and perpetrator to blame you and deny accountability for his actions.

Think about how Juno was the victim of her TBR. Yet, she ended up in jail because Larry intentionally and maliciously made false claims that Juno physically harmed him. Larry was a Machiavellian manipulator who made friends, family, and even the law believe that Juno was "the crazy perpetrator." Larry, like many ex-lovers, cried wolf.

I have worked with several women whose abusive partners make baseless accusations against them, and like Juno, the women end up in jail for a night or two. Other partners make false child abuse claims. The PL's continuation of gaslighting and false accusations can intensify your mental and physical trauma symptoms.

DARVO is a three-step method of twisting accountability and falsely accusing you. The DARVO process includes the PL denying, attacking, and switching the victim and perpetrator roles.[3]

1. **Deny.** The first step is for the PL to deny whatever wrongdoing he is accused of, such as stealing, cheating, lying to, abusing, or betraying you. The PL will refuse to take responsibility for any element of abuse he is accused of and remain steadfast in his claim.

Depending on the abuse in question, an abuser might say the following:

- "I never lied to/cheated on/hit/betrayed you."
- "How dare you accuse me of doing that!"
- "You're lying."
- "I'm a secure person. Why would I want to control you?"

2. **Attack.** After denials, the PL goes on the offensive and does everything to undermine you. He hate-bombs you as much as he love-bombed you. He "cries wolf" and launches false accusations. For instance, he might question your motivation, mental health, and stability and attack your intelligence, honesty, morality, and actions (past and present).

The PL attacks you with words in countless ways, including the following:

- "You're crazy."
- "You're a racist."
- "You're neglecting me and making me feel bad."
- "You're an alcoholic and a danger to the kids."
- "You're gaslighting me. You're the abuser."

- "You asked for this."
- "You are the problem. Our daughter never acts out at my house."

PLs also lie to therapists and lawyers, tell Child Protection Services you are harming their children, run smear campaigns, and try to brainwash your family and friends and turn the children against you.

3. **Reverse.** PLs attempt to use the old "switcheroo," DARVO's trickiest element, to switch roles with you. They redirect blame, accusing you of being the abuser. This reversal varies per the situation and accusation. The PL may say *you* are the abusive one who threw a wine glass at his head. He could also say you get angry due to mental health challenges, and he has begged you to get help. The PL may also say you are accusing him of abuse to fix your image, earn more money, or get full custody— what he is attempting to do.

The PL's malicious attempts need more proof, but that seems unimportant. PLs are expert liars, charmers, and manipulators. They will do anything to keep their status, money, and power. Remember, control is their primary goal.

HOW DARVO TAKES ITS TOLL

When your ex-PL uses DARVO, he co-opts a traumatizing event. He perpetuates the abusive and manipulative trauma bond even though you left him. One of the most devastating effects of DARVO is that you may doubt your memory and experience confusion about the events. Simultaneously, your children may experience trauma symptoms of anxiety and stomach pains because they feel they are put in the middle. You already have cognitive dissonance, so the

DARVO tactic only adds to your self-doubt. DARVO is gaslighting on steroids.

It can be very disheartening to finally escape your TBR and still get abused and harassed by your ex-PL. Here is how one of my patients described her symptoms from DARVO. Her ex-PL repeatedly called Child Protective Services and planted lies in her young children's minds. She explained to me,

> I feel like my body was in a car accident, achy yet combined with bouts of being frozen, lying around, and staring into space.
>
> I feel harassed at every level: I fear knocking at my door and phone calls. I cannot have normal relationships with men and women because people fear having Child Protective Services calls. The amount of effort it takes to stabilize our family unit takes away from being a mother. Why isn't this being viewed as emotional and psychological abuse of them and me?

HOW TO RESIST DARVO

Challenging, resisting, or combatting DARVO is possible. You will need to:

1. **Get educated.** Education is the first step in resisting DARVO. Simply learning about it can diminish its impact. Research shows that DARVO is less influential if you understand it.[4] For example, survivors who know about DARVO may be less likely to doubt themselves. Recognizing and naming DARVO can be a powerful antidote to getting tricked.

2. **Document the story.** One of the best things you can do is document your experience, including any accusations. Although

you may be reeling from the intense emotion of the situation, record the event's details, time, and location. This information will help you when you need clarification.

3. **Recognize the denial.** After the PL has denied the allegations, expect the next steps. This denial will signal their use of DARVO; from here, you can predict their next move.

4. **Identify and counter the attacks.** The attacks will follow closely behind the denial. They may play on your insecurities or regrets but remember that these are mainly untrue and invalid. Remind yourself that your PL can accuse you of many things. Since the accusations are not based on facts, eventually, the truth will emerge. In the meantime, don't allow their baseless attacks to get under your skin, and don't take them seriously. The PL wants an emotional reaction from you; he wants to push you over the edge, so don't give him that. Stay calm and use your emotional regulation skills.

5. **Avoid role reversal.** As your PL moves toward role reversal, do your best to state and restate your experience. Utilize the broken record technique, summarizing events in precisely the same way.

DARVO is a continuation of the emotional and psychological abuse you endured in your TBR. Now, though, you know the playbook. Expecting and understanding this abuse tactic will help you resist and recover from your TBR.

No Contact or Strategic Contact

As challenging as severing all contact may seem, it's the most viable path toward healing. Some survivors tried to straddle both worlds at first because even though they knew they couldn't have a healthy relationship, they could not imagine their life without their PL. Some survivors thought they could still be "friends" to honor those years of shared history and good memories. However, any form of contact feeds the trauma bond you are trying to sever. There is no such thing as "being friends" with a pathological person; this is a harsh reality you must accept after leaving. Staying friends is like having surgery to remove a cancerous tumor but leaving just a few cells behind; cancer will reinfect your body the same way your pathological "friend" will reinfect your life.

Implementing the no-contact rule after a breakup keeps a survivor safe and creates the necessary space for her to heal. She *must* take time away from her ex to gain perspective and work on herself. No contact is a firm boundary that finally allows the survivor to care for herself.

However, implementing no contact when you have children is not practical and can work against you in legal proceedings. Strategic contact, such as "gray rocking," is the intelligent alternative to no contact for situations where people have children together. Gray rocking is the strategy of staying calm and showing no emotions no matter how much your ex-PL insults, lies, or gaslights you. Also, you give your ex limited information and keep communication with him to a minimum.

The survivor and her ex can communicate through a co-parenting app such as OurFamilyWizard, which lets you and your ex keep financial records, share information (e.g., "The new babysitter's number is . . ."), and contribute to an online calendar for the kids' sake. Its "message board" function lets you and your ex chat about the kids and keep each other updated (e.g., "Leaving the birthday party now. Will have Sadie back to you within half an hour."). Also, with OurFamilyWizard, the abusive PL knows he is being watched, so he might behave better.

Whether to implement no contact or strategic contact is a decision you can make with the support of a therapist who is well trained in domestic violence or a divorce or family law attorney. Following these strategies will increase the outcome of a successful and safe exit from your trauma bond. Yet, as I mentioned at the start of this chapter, getting out is a process, and the trauma bond doesn't just magically dissipate once you're out. Let's be real. The PL wasn't nice or sympathetic when you were in a relationship with him, and he's certainly not going to be kind and thoughtful now that you've left him.

FREE AT LAST

As a therapist who has worked with and facilitated countless successful trauma bond exits, I can tell you that a survivor's euphoria is palpable when she is finally free. It is hard to imagine a release from prison that is more invigorating. Alex said if she had known she was going to feel "this alive," she would have left sooner. Lily said she hadn't been able to take a deep breath in over two years and spent several hours savoring the sensation of her lungs expanding fully. Survivors glow, imagining life's infinite possibilities. Every survivor I know has expressed how the outcome of freedom was worth the agony of the escape process. Freedom is a lifeline.

All survivors describe how good it feels to live without put-downs and pressure. Or they notice other people in the world respect them and treat them well. Without the PL to manipulate them, survivors start to think their thoughts. And they start to feel how truly peaceful and safe life is without their pathological torturer.

Yet, the feeling of being victimized is undeniable; survivors feel stripped of their sense of self. After enduring so much abuse, self-pity is tempting, but it does nothing for your healing and denies you your adult freedom. The good news is that 75 percent of people who experience trauma grow from it, especially women who have endured intimate partner violence.[5] There is hope. Part 3 teaches you how to recover from a trauma bond and become a *surthriver*.

KEY POINTS TO REMEMBER

1. Leaving a trauma bond is not simple. A survivor's safety is most at risk when she attempts to go, so successful and safe exits require a strategy and plan:

   - Never let them see you coming; once they know you're leaving, they will react unpredictably and violently, attack all sides, and put your safety at risk.

   - Prepare for violence by alerting friends, family, and the police; always try to end it in a public setting or with others present.

   - Seek legal counsel and document everything ahead of leaving.

   - Tell him when he's sober; drugs and alcohol make him more impulsive and put your safety at risk.

   - If there is a history of sexual violence, do not tell him unless you will no longer be residing in the same house. Telling him while you still live together can incite more sexual violence.

   - Prepare your finances, collect all necessary documents, prepare a bag of essentials, obtain a copy of all incriminating evidence, and delete anything that leaves you vulnerable.

   - Decide on and implement either no contact or strategic contact after consulting with a professional (especially when there are children involved).

2. After leaving a trauma bond, survivors must prepare for:

   - Overwhelming feelings of fear and disloyalty due to prolonged abuse.

   - Stalking and increased violence, which should be well documented and are grounds for a restraining order.

   - DARVO, a three-step method of twisting accountability and

falsely accusing you. The DARVO process is deny, attack, and reverse victim and offender.

- The need for professional help from a licensed, trauma-informed clinician—not a church counselor, spiritual coach, or life coach. Seeking help from an unqualified or underqualified person is a traumatizing experience and can exacerbate your symptoms and cause more damage. Resources for finding appropriate services are available at the end of this book.

3. Survivors experience a mix of euphoria and victimization upon finally being free from their trauma bond. They are faced with the decision to wallow in self-pity or heal. The good news is that 75 percent of people experience post-traumatic growth!

PART 3

The Wisdom of the Wound

8 Post-Traumatic Growth

You, in particular, have so much to be proud of,
so much that you've done well in the face of adversity.
And the strengths you have are just beginning to flourish.[1]

—LUNDY BANCROFT

SO, I KNOW THIS MIGHT sound crazy, but I believe that after healing from your trauma bond, you can experience post-traumatic growth. Richard G. Tedeschi and Lawrence Calhoun coined *post-traumatic growth (PTG)*.[2] PTG describes the personal evolution you can experience after IPV. Seventy-five percent of people who experience trauma will grow from it (a trauma statistic we never hear). They become healthier and improve in their next life phase. PTG doesn't deny deep distress but suggests adversity can positively change a life. Hope is hard to come by after surviving a TBR, but having scientific literature rooting for your recovery is precisely what you need!

In their research, Tedeschi and Calhoun describe, transformative changes that occur gradually.[3] Women can gain a more profound appreciation for themselves knowing they survived brutal domination and manipulation. After enduring IPV, they have learned what they will not tolerate, which enables them to have healthier connections. After rediscovering their authentic self, they can explore new interests that give their lives meaning and purpose. Often, their relationships with spirituality deepen. Triumphing after a TBR and trying to make sense of it can lead to robust personal growth.

Creating meaning from your suffering also supports PTG. Suffering becomes significant when you use your trauma to become wiser, more loving, and whole. I am not saying everything happens for a reason because that would be toxic positivity. I am stating that you can use your pain to inspire growth. It takes time to trust that anything so tormenting can add value to your life. Stay open to the possibility of gaining insight from your soul-shattering trauma bond.

Finding meaning was important in Alex's recovery after her marriage to Tom. We explored how her unknown personality traits made her vulnerable to control and abuse. She realized that her agreeableness initially motivated her to trust Tom. And then, when he lied, her cooperativeness kicked in, and to keep the peace, she did not make a big deal about it. Tom's dominating behavior and Alex's compliant nature caused her to disconnect from her values and needs. Her tolerant personality and optimism made her hopeful that he would change. She also realized how her caretaking made her life chaotic. Alex learned that her prosocial personality was weaponized against her by Tom, and she vowed never to sacrifice her safety and sanity in the name of love. These are just a few lessons she developed that guide her life today.

However, nobody has the right to tell you your painful TBR happened for a reason. The meaning you take from your TBR must be your choice and feel right for you. A TBR is life-altering; it is not a life sentence.

This chapter provides different action steps to support your PTG. And because of TBR's unique impact, this section provides specialized skills needed to recover from the trauma symptoms of loss of self, cognitive dissonance, and C-PTSD. Just like traumatic bonding is a destructive process, healing is a therapeutic process. Recovering from traumatic bonding will require effort, practice, and commitment. To begin your recovery, it is necessary to feel safe and stable, so if you feel triggered during this process, please use the following grounding technique below to help you calm yourself.

Grounding refers to using your ability to sense your body and feel your feet on the earth to calm your nervous system. Grounding is a crucial skill for emotional overwhelm. Your senses (hearing, seeing, smelling, tasting, and touching) are the only necessary tools for anchoring yourself in the present moment. A straightforward practice involves naming five things you see, four things you hear, three things you can touch, two things you can smell, and then taking one deep, slow breath.[4]

Grounding is an effective skill to rely on during your recovery process whenever you feel triggered. Also, finding a therapist, embracing self-care, and not retelling your story over and over will support your emotional stabilization. Let's jump in!

FIND A GOOD THERAPIST TO SUPPORT YOU

The most critical advice I can give any survivor is to get professional help and support. The process of healing should not occur in isolation, as isolation makes you vulnerable. Once you decide to leave, regular contact with a professional is essential because there may be many false starts, changes of plans, and vows to leave that get postponed. Having support keeps you accountable and safe.

I hope by now it is evident that survivors have experienced profound trauma. Traumatic relationships are frightening and overwhelming; without healing the trauma, you're prone to falling right back into another pathological relationship. Not all therapists are created equally, meaning that not all therapists are trauma-trained or have adequate education in domestic violence. Therefore, you must hire a trauma therapist. Luckily, there are many more trauma-trained therapists and modalities today than in my day.

Too many women have told me, "My other therapist didn't get it. She told me I was an enabler." Or they have gone to their church counselor who tried to get them to stay with or return to the psychopath. Hear me when I say this: church counselors, spiritual coaches, and life coaches are not licensed or trained professionals. Seeking help from an unqualified or underqualified person is a traumatizing experience and can exacerbate your symptoms and cause more damage. It takes a well-trained therapist with professional knowledge of domestic violence to assist survivors. For this reason, I have included a list of resources that will direct you to competent care.

That said, the connection you share with a therapist is crucial to your healing success. A large part of healing occurs simply through the experience of having a healthy and safe relationship with another human. So, if you find a therapist that isn't an expert in TBRs but you feel safe with them, I am sure they would be open to learning. Recovery is possible when survivors make the right choice about treatment. Now I recognize that getting a trauma-trained therapist is not always feasible due to money and accessibility issues. That is why I am offering tools in this book to support you in this deeply rewarding healing journey.

SELF-CARE: THE ROYAL ROAD TO HEALING

Being in a TBR where you are intimidated and threatened weekly causes you to feel unsafe. A major step in recovering is feeling safe enough to do the healing. To begin recovery, it is essential to feel emotionally and psychologically stable.[5] This section explains self-care practices to create safety so you can embark on your healing journey.

The price of admission into a TBR is sacrificing all your needs and desires. A pathological person's self-centered actions come from the greedy pursuit of meeting his needs for power and pleasure. In a TBR, he demands all your attention and time and then complains that you ignore him. He intimidates you into tolerating his abuse and addictions. Or manipulates you and requires you to help him with a project, making you neglect your responsibilities while calling you a lazy piece of shit. Selfless sacrifice might make you feel like the partner, wife, or girlfriend of the year, yet repeatedly neglecting yourself hurts you. People-pleasing is an effective way of stopping or avoiding arguments. Yet, it is an unsustainable tactic to make your partner love you more or behave.

For example, Alex erased her personality and abandoned her career and connections with her friends and family to keep Tom's love. In the end, nothing she did was ever good enough for him. High-achieving Lily passed up opportunities and sacrificed her college experience to keep up with Jason's wild lifestyle. She knew she could never pursue her goals and have him as a partner, but she stuck around anyway. Every time he hurt her, she ignored her pain to help him process his, hoping her love and loyalty would do the trick. Alex and Lily met their partner's needs at their expense, hurting them in the end. They neglected themselves.

Healthy self-care or selfishness doesn't mean you don't care for others, nor is it an immoral characteristic. People with healthy narcissism consider and respect their happiness, needs, and freedom while connecting with their lovers.[6] This is the opposite of traumatic bonding, which demands you abandon yourself to keep your relationship. By not neglecting yourself, you are cherishing yourself—an act of self-love.

Healthy self-care means putting yourself first. Did your whole body cringe reading that? You have been in a relationship where you were treated as an object and an afterthought, not a priority or an equal. So, learning to prioritize yourself is the first and foremost step to healing; you must put your needs first to find balance and recover from the trauma of your bond. This is not to say you become narcissistic, self-centered, rigid, or rude—you can put yourself first and still be considerate and compassionate toward others. However, recovery from a TBR requires compassion toward yourself first and foremost. Your TBR might be over, but are other relationships in your life requiring you to belittle yourself and accommodate others' needs first? These relationships are a great place to start implementing your pressing self-care needs.

You hoped you would feel better after leaving, and maybe part of you does, yet you also get overwhelmed by fear, anger, and shame. Survivors often use food, drugs, and alcohol to avoid feeling their overwhelming pain and loneliness. Juno explained how two weeks before she came to therapy, she mixed Xanax and alcohol (which should never be mixed) and ended up in the hospital. She needed relief from the agony of Larry's cheating, manipulation, and abandonment.

Drugs and alcohol give you immediate relief, yet in the long run, they hurt you more. If you or the people who care about you believe you are excessively numbing with drugs and alcohol, please let your therapist know or try attending a 12-step meeting. Not because your therapist or group tells you to stop, but because social support is usually the missing ingredient that leads to substance use. Keeping your harmful coping mechanisms hidden creates more shame, which drives you further into the behavior and stops your recovery. You have already lived through enough emotional torture, and your abuser is gone. Do not fill his shoes and begin abusing yourself because you've become accustomed to that reality. Choose to be kind to yourself by being with and nurturing those hurting parts.

Similarly, spending sprees, compulsively working, filling all your free time with friends, or Netflix, or overexercising do initially soothe your overwhelming loneliness. These distractions give you strong hits of dopamine, the feel-good neurotransmitter, yet they don't support your recovery. Learning to be with your feelings and manage them is crucial for healing. (Strategies for that are explained in a bit.)

Self-care becomes effective when you repeat health-promoting behaviors until they become habits. As a somatic therapist, I often tell my patients, "You don't have a body; you are your body." Mental and physical health are not separate things. Newsflash: your mind (brain) is part of your body. Therefore, you are one integrated system. So, attend to your body's needs and establish healthy habits to support your physical well-being, which will contribute to feeling mentally and emotionally balanced.

MOVEMENT AND YOGA

One particularly effective tool for healing trauma is yoga.[7] Yoga is not a religion; it is a philosophy and science. Numerous research indicates yoga's physical, emotional, and mental health benefits. Unlike other forms of exercise, yoga's focus is inward. The chaotic mind becomes calm by connecting breath to movement. And your breath is a free tool always available to link your mind and body so you can soothe your nerves. The more you experience a calm nervous system, the more traumatic imprints on the body slowly dissipate. Also, emotions are held in the body (more on this later). Yoga, like massage, is specifically designed to release muscle tension and gently release emotion. It is not uncommon to release emotions on your yoga mat. Most yoga instructors expect this to happen.

So, go to yoga, even when you don't want to. Showing up is the hardest part, yet I guarantee you will never walk out of a yoga class saying, "I wish I hadn't come today." Try out different studios or start with free YouTube videos. Try different styles and instructors or google "yoga for trauma." The more you get into your body through mindful movement, the more aware you will become of your needs—your tiredness, hunger, loneliness, peace, and anxiety. Feeling safe is the first step, putting yourself first is the second, knowing what you need is third, and acting on those needs is next.

NUTRITION

Many patients describe their intention to eat healthy, nourishing foods. Yet, after a long day, they reward themselves with a glass of wine, a couple of chocolates, some spoonfuls of ice cream, a bag of chips, or some unhealthy fast food. Or if their ex harasses them, healthy intentions fly out the window. Next thing they know, they can't get food down their throat fast enough. To soothe their pain, they binge-eat in front of the TV. After several weeks, their clothes suddenly don't fit right. They hate how they feel, and now they hate how they look—double whammy. I remember when Lily broke up with Jason, every time I FaceTimed her to check in, she was snacking on chips or cheese, no matter what time of day. I later found out she had eaten an entire family-size pack of Cheez-Its and two French baguettes in just one day. Not only does binging postpone your healing, but it also poisons your body and makes you feel lethargic, depressed, and anxious.

Food is a highly soothing substance that is incredibly easy to obtain. I know how difficult it is to make healthy choices when you feel like you're emotionally rotting from the inside out. So, start small. Try having one nutritious meal daily, breakfast to start your day off right, or grab a salad for lunch or dinner. Swap your snacks and binge foods for healthier options—instead of Cheetos, try visiting Whole Foods or Trader Joe's for slightly more nutritious alternatives. Instead of Reese's Pieces, Snickers Bars, and Kit-Kats, go for dark chocolate from the grocery store or some fresh peanut butter. The point is to balance your urge to binge and your body's need for nutrients.

Ultimately, adhering to a nutrient-rich diet and workout plan are loving actions. Self-care and maturity involve delaying instant gratification. It's not all chocolates and bubble baths. It includes pausing your impulse for cookie dough ice cream and making a more conscious decision. Having discipline is how you can master being a responsible adult. Remember, the root word of discipline is "disciple," which means love. Hence, mature self-care is having the discipline to act on what is in your best interest long-term.

Again, treat your body with respect like you would with any living being reliant on you for their health. Follow the advice you give your daughter, son, or best friend. See a psychiatrist if your anxiety or depression is too challenging to manage. Go for a walk if you haven't been out of the house in a while. Alex said that religiously going for a walk every morning stabilized her. Make your bed and clean your home if it looks like a bomb has gone off. Stop staying up late and sleeping in till 11 a.m. Go back to the basics: nourishing food, adequate sleep, daily movement, trauma therapy, and medications. These are all effective resources to encourage healing.

Resistance to new behaviors does not mean they are wrong; they are new and foreign. You may feel awkward or uncomfortable, but it's okay. That's completely normal when you're trying something new. Nurturing yourself daily provides a corrective caring experience for your precious self. You grew accustomed to being completely neglected and abused. Creating internal safety with self-care will allow you to revisit your TBR in a supportive way so you can recover from it and grow.

Self-Care Reflection Questions

1. Do you know what personality traits caused you to believe you must sacrifice your needs, values, and desires to be loved?

2. Journal prompt: What if being loved does not mean I have to sacrifice my needs? What does that bring up for me?

3. Can you commit to at least one self-care action daily to recover from your TBR? If so, which one? If not, why?

4. Daily questions to ask for the next two weeks (at least):
   - What do I need today?

Self Care
EVERYDAY

SUNDAY

MONDAY

TUESDAY

WEDNESDAY

THURSDAY

FRIDAY

SATURDAY

Meditation | Breathwork

Mindfulness | Spiritual Practices

Hobbies | Projects

Sleep | Sleeping In | Sleeping Early

Healthy Eating | Meal Prepping

Exercise (Yoga, Hiking, Home Workouts, Etc)

Baths | Cold Plunges

Heating Pads | Weighted Blankets

Candles or Diffusers | Aromatherapy

Cleaning & Organizing

Being Outdoors | Visiting the Ocean

Therapy | Support Groups

Coloring | Painting

Knitting | Sewing

Morning or Evening Walks

Cooking | Baking

Self Pampering | Massage

Listening or Playing Music

Dance | Movement

Reading | Learning | Webinars

Social Connection | Being with Loved Ones

Spending Time with Pets

Being of Service to Others

Credit: L. Friedman-Gell and J. Barron, *Intergenerational Trauma Workbook Strategies to Support Your Journey of Discovery, Growth, and Healing* (Rockridge Press, 2020), p. 118.

- What is one thing I will do today to nourish my body?

- What is one thing I will do today to nourish my mind?

- What is one thing I will do today to nourish my spirit/soul?

5. How do you imagine your life can change with better self-care?

6. What emotional support do you have? Friends, trauma-informed support groups, therapy?

YOU ARE NOT YOUR STORY

The trauma symptom of CD causes a compulsive need to tell and retell your story to reconcile what happened. Constantly narrating your story triggers panic and destabilizes you. You walk around in a constant state of anxiety and hypervigilance from thinking about the horrific abuse you endured. Even though you left your PL, your body acts as if he lurks around every corner, creating lasting stress after your TBR.

If the harm from surviving TBR isn't bad enough, some things will cause trauma symptoms to worsen. You have a terrible, crazy story and a good reason to share it. The realization of being used and abused would make anyone want to shout the truth from the rooftops. Trust me; I understand that you want to get validation for the insanity you survived. According to Sandra L. Brown, MA, survivors believe getting confirmation of their twisted romance will lessen their CD.[8] However, chronic storytelling is not an effective way to heal—it's an effective way to retraumatize yourself. The number one rule of trauma therapy is "never ask the patient to tell you their trauma story" for this reason.

I empathize with your longing to hear other women's stories and speak your truth. However, recovery requires being cautious about when and with whom you communicate; you must protect yourself. When you share the details of your TBR, you risk becoming triggered, causing the distressing emotions and thoughts from the abuse to destabilize you emotionally. Yet, stability is what you need most during recovery. Revisiting your toxic experience is essential. However, you should process it when you are emotionally supported and have the skills to manage your symptoms. Recounting your narrative within a controlled setting, such as with your therapist or in a support group run by a trauma-trained therapist, is essential.

Blogs and Internet sites that are not trauma-informed encourage survivors to read disturbing posts and disclose their trauma narratives. Watching shows or movies depicting abuse or trauma bonds is also retraumatizing. Social media is rife with survivor-turned-expert's psychology accounts. As a rule, you should take everything you read on social media with a grain of salt. Also, not all social media accounts are trauma-informed, which means that while their content is good, it might not apply to you now.

Furthermore, online programs are not always run by therapists with advanced training in psychology, personality traits, and, most relevant, psychopathology. So, while the intentions of all these resources are good, it is essential to receive psychological support from professionals academically educated on how to treat trauma. This is because you are in a highly vulnerable state mentally and emotionally, and not receiving the proper help can delay, not promote, your recovery.

Keri described how she found a narcissist survivor's support group with weekly online meetings. She recalled her first group session: Every woman's story made her feel reassaulted. Her throat tightened, her heart raced, and she panicked and closed her screen. She had insomnia as endless thoughts about Nick's drunken abuse and images of his Grindr texts were on repeat in her mind. She stayed up all night, curled up in bed, staring at the ceiling. Hence, what she thought would be soothing and validating was traumatizing and undermining her recovery.

Research shows that exposing yourself to uninformed trauma care can interfere with your successful recovery.[9] Getting emotionally hijacked repeatedly is unhelpful. So, to avoid experiencing more psychological injury, use the resources below to guide your recovery. If you work with a therapist, please have them check out the sites you visit. Or send them the resources you find and ask them what they think. You want to do everything to support your recovery.

TRAUMA-TRAINED TREATMENTS TO SUPPORT YOUR RECOVERY

1. Eye Movement Desensitization and Reprocessing (EMDR) is a psychotherapy treatment initially designed to alleviate the distress associated with traumatic memories.

2. Somatic Experiencing (SE) is a body-oriented therapeutic model that helps heal trauma and other stress disorders.

3. Brainspotting is a powerful, focused treatment method that identifies, processes, and releases core sources of trauma.

4. The NeuroAffective Relational Model (NARM) is a cutting-edge mind-body model for addressing relational and developmental trauma by working with the attachment patterns causing interpersonal difficulties.

5. Internal Family Systems (IFS) is a transformative model of psychotherapy that works with our inner parts and core self.

6. Emotional Freedom Technique (EFT) is a mind-body method of tapping acupuncture points (acupoints) on the hands, face, and body with your fingertips while focusing on an issue or feeling you hope to resolve.

7. Sensorimotor Psychotherapy (SP) is a therapeutic modality for trauma and attachment issues utilizing the mind, body, and spirit.

8. *Safe Relationships Magazine* provides a safe place for survivors
   to access trauma-trained therapists who specialize in TBRs.

DISSOLVE COGNITIVE DISSONANCE

Now that you understand ways to support yourself in feeling stable during your recovery, let's explore a specific skill to help you heal. Chronic
and persistent cognitive dissonance (CD) is a long-term condition not
often reduced by leaving your TBR. While healing is not linear, CD
needs to be addressed early so you can dissolve the very mechanism
that held your trauma bond together.

CD affects your executive functioning (EF) skills. Remember, EF
skills are concentration, memory, decision-making, rational judgment,
and planning, all of which you need to stay away from your ex-PL,
plan for your future, and organize your new life. Also, judgment errors
can interfere with self-care and healthy decisions. Moreover, when you
can't reason, you will have difficulty resisting your PL's promises. He
claims he will undergo therapy, attend Sex Addicts Anonymous, and
never drink again. Therefore, starting to dissolve your CD is essential
to success in recovery-oriented behaviors.

You have CD because of your PL's two personas: Dr. Jekyll/Mr.
Hyde. You have categorized the conflicting experiences, opposing
emotions, and contrasting beliefs: "He's a generous love-bomber who I
love and can trust and a selfish abuser who I resent and can't trust." It's
as if you have been in a relationship with two people.

Sandra L. Brown, MA, and her researchers created a link-and-label
technique to reduce your CD over time. This technique is a way of
connecting something that happened, its consequences, and its cause.
Creating and holding connections can be tricky when you have been
manipulated and lied to. Also, you became disconnected from reality
due to chronic gaslighting.

Yet, you already know the labels of your personality and your partner's, as well as the terms that describe his behaviors and the results. So,

once you can connect the cause of your experiences and pain (pathology exposure) and its effects on you (trauma and CD symptoms), you begin to integrate your experience. You can label your PL's pathology (cause) and link how his behavior traumatized you (effect). And your tender-mindedness (cause) supported your tolerance (effect) of his behaviors. These aha moments help integrate your experiences. Your thoughts and feelings about your PL are no longer compartmentalized, which is the beginning of reducing CD.

Here are some examples:

- Label of his personality (the cause) and link pathological behavior (the effect).
- Your PL's narcissism and psychopathy result in grandiosity and pathological lying.
- Label your personality (the cause) and link it with your tolerant behavior (the effect)
- Due to your agreeableness, you tolerated his claims that he would change.
- Label his gaslighting behavior (the cause) and link it to you feeling confused (the effect).
- Your ex denied cheating with your friend despite you finding explicit photos of her on his phone. He gaslighted you, telling you that you were paranoid, and now you are confused.

The link-and-label technique enables you to make connections between everything you have learned about trauma bonds. When you make those connections regularly, your CD starts to lessen. As you reduce CD, your thoughts are less fragmented and take up less space in your brain; hence, you ruminate less, leaving you time to concentrate, make healthy decisions, and plan your future.

FIND YOURSELF AGAIN
WITH MINDFULNESS

Your PL systematically tore you down and stripped you of your power. You lost your sense of self and individuality. Being controlled by an intimate dictator causes you to forfeit connection to yourself, so you self-abandon. Chronic CD confuses you, and you behave in ways against your core values. You wind up becoming a shadow of your former self. You lose trust in your ability to reason. You can't depend on yourself to make decisions anymore. You don't know who you are. However, in this chapter, you learn the self-reflection skill of mindfulness to connect with the truth inside of you and get back in the driver's seat of your life so you can feel empowered to act on your behalf. This section will help you connect to your authentic self.

Your PL's controlling ways forced you to ignore your authentic self daily while in your TBR. So, to stop self-abandoning, you must commit to looking inward and listening to yourself again. You must learn the skill of self-reflection. Self-reflection is pausing and pondering your feelings, thoughts, and reactions. Self-reflection allows you to see the "big picture" of your inner landscape.

Self-reflection is a mindfulness practice. Mindfulness is the awareness that arises through purposefully paying attention to yourself in the present moment. You witness your reactions calmly and curiously. It's a way of slowing down, connecting with your inner world, and responding mindfully to the situation.

Mindfulness requires that you connect with your inner witness to observe yourself. This part of you can pause and watch your thoughts and feelings. Your inner observer does not judge or comment on your experience. Its job is to intentionally observe what you think, feel, say, and do in the present. Your inner observer needs the invitation to come forward.

For example, even though Keri divorced Nick, she eventually faced Nick regarding their daughters' schedules and needs. Nick always ignored their custody agreement and wanted the girls whenever it suited his schedule. When Keri disagreed, he threatened her. Keri told me how she would get triggered and sometimes rage back at him or occasionally yield to him. So, we worked on the reactions she would have upon receiving an email from Nick; she would pause, take a breath, and take notice of what she was thinking and feeling in the present moment. Often, she felt like she was inside a tornado. Her thoughts would be, "He's such a controlling asshole" or "I fear his temper, and I can't deal with him."

Once she learned the skill of mindfulness, she would not judge her thoughts but witness them float by. Then she would pause, take some breaths to calm her nervous system, and connect to her authentic thoughts and feelings about how she wanted to handle his email. Sure enough, he demanded to see the girls one day, even though it was not on the schedule. She paused and checked in with herself; she agreed because it worked for her and the girls, and that response to Nick felt right. She was not reacting or giving in; she responded from her authentic self. Using her mind to control her brain felt empowering.

I know you had to override your genuine feelings and needs in your TBR. Yet learning the skill of connecting to your inner witness is a mindfulness practice that will help you recover your lost self. At first, it might feel awkward, like when you get a new pair of shoes and they give you blisters. However, if you commit to the practice, you will see that it comes more naturally over time. And since power is the ability to influence yourself, mindfulness is a way to feel authentically empowered.

How to Cultivate Your Inner Observer

Learning the skill of mindfulness requires practice. If you wanted to learn how to play a song on the piano, you would have to practice it daily till it became second nature. The same applies to using your inner observer. So, here are some steps to practice when you have time so that when you get triggered after your TBR or by your PL, you have some skills that will allow you to respond mindfully. Like any skill, the more you do it, the better you will get at it.

1. Hit the pause button on anything you are doing right now.

2. Recruit your inner observer and notice what you are experiencing in the present moment.

3. Notice your thoughts: Are they about the past or future? Or about your ex? Don't judge what comes to mind. Let the thoughts float by.

4. Again, focus on the present moment by concentrating on your breath going through your nose and out through your mouth.

5. Let distractions come and go and stay as focused as you can on your breath and being in the present moment, nothing else.

6. When you feel calm or relaxed, reengage in life.

7. If you need to make a decision, make it now from this calm, centered, authentic state.

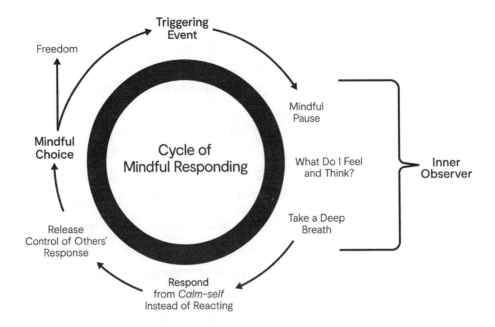

BOUNDARIES

Setting boundaries is impossible with a PL whose primary mission is to have power over you. Pathological partners are forceful, controlling, and invasive; they have no boundaries and certainly don't respect anyone else's. They dominate your life and push their agenda forward, regardless of how you feel or what you say. Setting limits with them about the littlest things is impossible, let alone the big stuff. PLs hate boundaries because limits get in the way of meeting their selfish needs for comfort, power, and pleasure.

In a TBR, boundary violations might start small, but they snowball to the point of total domination. Your partner criticizes you when you wash the dishes differently than he does, so you decide to do it his way. Then, perhaps you realize you have health issues and need to adjust the foods you eat. He calls you dramatic for eating gluten-free, even though your health requires it. He rolls his eyes when you request modifications at a restaurant. So, you give in and silently suffer the consequences. Until you are free from the relationship and able to focus solely on yourself, you don't realize the extent to which you self-abandoned.

Learning the skill of setting boundaries will help you stop self-abandonment and is another practice to help you regain your sense of self. Once you can mindfully connect to your inner world, you will know what you authentically feel, think, and need. Boundaries are the emotional and mental separations you need to feel safe, valued, and respected in a relationship.[10] And you set your boundaries by clearly expressing your expectations and needs. Setting a boundary requires you to voice your "no" to say "yes" to you. Once you decide on a boundary reinforcement, you might have to repeat yourself several times.

Understanding how to develop and implement your limits is a life skill for relationships. Fluid boundaries are flexible enough to have intimate connections with others while still staying true to yourself. The key is to strike a balance between your needs and the needs of others. And keeping boundaries means accepting that you cannot always please the other person—and that's okay. Because when you maintain boundaries, you show yourself and others that you value and respect yourself.

See if any of these boundary styles resonate with you: If you allow your lover to yell and dominate you or repeatedly lie, you might have an *unbounded boundary style.* You initially welcome your PL's bold confidence. "How nice to have a man that takes charge." Eventually, you wind up losing all your rights. Survivors who score high in agreeableness are willing to compromise, so they lose personal boundaries over time because they give in to the PL's threats. Even if you know how you feel and what you want, maintaining a boundary line—especially once you've been submissive to his decisions—can be very challenging with an intimidating maniac.

If you tend to withdraw when in conflict with your lover, you have a *rigid boundary style.* You might feel safest when you are self-reliant. When your lover breaks your boundaries, you shut down and become disconnected, cold, noncommunicative, and aloof. For example, Keri would tell Nick not to have drinks before he picked up their daughter. Ignoring her, Nick would come home drunk. Then Keri would get angry, and Nick would say, "Shut up! What are you so fuckin' mad about? You make a big deal out of everything." Keri explained that she would walk away, get into bed, and pretend she was sleeping when he entered the bedroom. She just wanted the attacks to stop.

A survivor with a rigid boundary style might find it challenging to share themselves emotionally with their partner. Your self-reliance and bond to a selfish lover make it doubly harder to express yourself. Living with a self-centered PL can make your "stay away" boundaries even more rigid because it confirms the belief that you must take care of things yourself. Yet being self-sufficient triggers your PL's insecurity; he screams, "You're a self-centered bitch," which raises your emotional walls. The most common boundary style is a combination of the previous styles.

Healing involves self-awareness about your values, what you stand for, and what you will not sacrifice. Consider these your new relational rules—your integrity in black and white. When you stand up for yourself by upholding relational boundaries, you protect rather than abandon yourself. The opposite of abandonment is the commitment to your needs, feelings, and values. A sure way to develop self-esteem is repeatedly telling others what you will and will not tolerate. Writing out your values, personal manifesto, or relational rules is essential. Here is a sample from one of my patients; please use it as a guide to create yours.

I trust that I have power over my life and, in doing so, accept full responsibility for my experience in this life.

I request that others accept full responsibility for their experiences if they want to be in a relationship with me.

I know those who have harmed me can only make a sincere change if I remove myself from their harm. I acknowledge that the most loving thing I can do for myself is to no longer tolerate cruel or controlling behavior and insults.

I can choose who, what, and how to use my energy. I now choose to believe it is safe to be my authentic self. I trust myself to recover when I get it "wrong."

I have the power and the right to choose who I am energetically, emotionally, and spiritually tied to. I will only lend my energy to those who consistently show themselves safe, supportive, and sincere.

I vow to practice connecting to my authentic self so I can trust my deeper instincts fiercely.

I accept what has happened, learn from the past, and release myself from the burden of saving others. I no longer dance the dance of human sacrifice.

I vow to give myself what I give to others and to deny myself my deepest needs no longer.

You are you, and I am I. I am not in this world to be a vessel for you. I am my person, and I call back all my resources, love, power, and energy. I unhook myself from you and my need for validation from you. I am cutting the cord for good and trusting you on your journey so I can focus on mine.

When you stand up for yourself by upholding relational boundaries, you protect rather than abandon yourself. The opposite of abandonment is the commitment to your needs, feelings, and values. One of my patients described how she set a boundary with a friend who was in contact with her abusive ex-PL: "I cannot be friends with a person associated with a man who has emotionally and physically abused me. So, you can be friends with him, yet I am choosing to end our friendship." She protected herself by setting a clear boundary. Being able to state and enforce your personal "no" is empowering.

CONTAINING EMOTIONS THAT STRIKE LIKE LIGHTNING

The roller coaster nature of a TBR means you might feel hopeful in the morning since you had amazing make-up sex last night. But by midmorning, your PL is angry again for no reason, so now you feel frustrated, confused, and anxious. Later in the afternoon, you feel irritable due to your repressed anger and soothe yourself with cookie dough ice cream. By dinnertime, once the sugar high has worn off, you feel lonely because your PL is out with the boys again. To numb your sadness, you pour yourself one glass of chardonnay, but instead, you down the bottle. Now, you feel ashamed and overwhelmed, so you turn on Netflix and pass out.

This scenario illustrates emotional dysregulation, a typical trauma symptom.[11] When your feelings control your behavior, and you later regret what you did, you were emotionally dysregulated. And since you are used to feeling crazy, impulsive, or out of control due to your TBR, you need to learn how to manage your emotions.

You feel emotionally hijacked when strong emotions such as fear, anger, or anxiety overpower your intentional thoughts and behaviors. All too often, people describe emotions as "irrational." Indeed, they do not stem from the same processes as rational thinking, but emotions have their logic. Being blinded by anger, for example, may seem stupid. However, anger is a logical response to feeling threatened by an emotional bully. But if you bottle up your anger, the pressure builds and suddenly erupts. Outbursts of anger are counterproductive because people reject what you are asking for, and you act just like your ex-PL.

My goal is to teach you emotional regulation: how to manage your emotions effectively. An essential skill in your recovery is learning to express your feelings in a situationally appropriate way. The purpose is not to eliminate your emotions but to use mindful awareness to help you tolerate strong emotions without acting them out or repressing them. This section teaches you how to be mindfully present with and understand your feelings and their intentions.

Feeling overpowered by your emotions puts you at their mercy. I tell my patients, "Your ego lives in your mind, but your authentic self lives in your body." Therefore, your genuine emotions arise from your body's core. You feel your feelings through various physical sensations in your body's midline—the throat, heart, chest, and stomach. For example, sadness and grief are typically felt in the throat, shame in the chest, and social anxiety in the stomach.

There are three steps in developing the skill of emotional containment:[12]

1. The first is **somatic mindfulness**, which entails paying attention to your body's sensations to clarify which emotion you feel. Identifying your feelings is essential to managing them. To identify your feelings, use your inner observer and focus on your body's midline, from your throat to your pelvis. Pause and have your inner observer track your physical sensations—paying attention to your body is a way to be present with your feelings and not run from them. Name what you are feeling without judgment. Connecting your bodily sensations helps you feel grounded in your emotions, not blinded by them. For help with this, refer to the upcoming chart correlating emotions with bodily sensations.

2. The second step is to get **curious about your feelings**. What is that emotion trying to communicate to you? Why are you feeling angry right now? What is your sadness trying to tell you? What are you terrified of? What is the intention of your fear? Fear, anger, and sadness are not just ideas but essential, deep physical reactions. Please do not minimize, reject, or judge your feelings. Many people bypass their emotions through toxic positivity (keeping your vibration high). Denying your feelings means noticing them but refusing to face or process their meaning. Judging your feelings is extremely harmful—it's hard enough to experience painful emotions, so don't compound that pain with self-judgment.

PRIMARY EMOTION
Joy

SECONDARY EMOTIONS
cheerfulness, zest, contentment, pride, optimism, enthrallment, relief, amusement, bliss, glee, delight, enjoyment, gladness, happiness, elation, satisfaction, euphoria, enthusiasm, excitement

PHYSICAL SENSATIONS
expanded, electric, flowing, fluttery, radiating, spacious, tingling, vibrating, worm

PRIMARY EMOTION
Sadness

SECONDARY EMOTIONS
lonely, hurt, hurting, unhappy, gloomy, overwhelmed, distant, discouraged, distressed, dismayed, disheartened, despairing, sorrowful, depressed, blue, miserable,

PHYSICAL SENSATIONS
blocked, cold, drained, empty, frozen, heavy, hollow, knotted, nauseous, numb, pained, sensitive, sore

PRIMARY EMOTION
Anger

SECONDARY EMOTIONS
impatient, irritated, frustrated, grouchy, agitated, exasperated, disgusted, animosity, bitter, rancorous, irate, furious, angry, hostile, enraged

PHYSICAL SENSATIONS
burning, clenching, hot, pounding, prickly, tight, bulging, trembling, vibrating

PRIMARY EMOTION
Fear

SECONDARY EMOTIONS
afraid, startled, frightened, insecure, anguished, sensitive, shocked, jealous, terrified, horrified, desperate, helplessness, alarm, shock, panic

PHYSICAL SENSATIONS
breathless, clenched, constricted, frozen, knotted, nauseous, jumpy, pounding, sweaty, tense, tight, twitchy, wobbly

PRIMARY EMOTION
Shame

SECONDARY EMOTIONS
Embarrassed, humiliated, flawed, worthlessness, broken, weak, powerlessness, discomfort, pain, mortified

PHYSICAL SENSATIONS
blocked, burning chest, clenched, constricted, frozen, pulsing, shaky, sweaty, vibrating

PRIMARY EMOTION
Disgust

SECONDARY EMOTIONS
contempt, disdain, scorn, aversion, distaste, revulsion, disapproval, awful, repelled, judgmental, appalled, revolted, detestable, hesitant

PHYSICAL SENSATIONS
clenched, constricted, queasy, pulsing, shaky, tight

PRIMARY EMOTION
Surprise

SECONDARY EMOTIONS
amazement, astonishment, startled, confused, excited, shocked, dismayed, disillusioned, perplexed, astonished, awe, eager, energetic

PHYSICAL SENSATIONS
breathless, buzzed, electric, expanded, fluttery, jumpy, pulsing, radiating, tingly, shivering

PRIMARY EMOTION
Interest

SECONDARY EMOTIONS
attentive, undivided, absorbed, curious, engrossed, inquisitiveness, engaged, delighted, enjoyment

PHYSICAL SENSATIONS
buzzing, tension, vibration quickened heart rate, energetic

Understanding what fueled your sentiment allows you to put your efforts where needed.

3. The third step is to **contain your emotions**. Recovery involves reclaiming a sense of choice about how you manage your feelings. For example, you might feel intense grief after a TBR. Perhaps you experience it during your first holiday without your PL. You may notice a lump in your throat and heaviness in your chest. Be present with the physical sensation of your grief. Pause and get curious about why you feel sorrow. Perhaps you knew the TBR had to end, but you are grieving the loss of a life you imagined. Or maybe you are sad about the years you feel have been wasted by your TBR. Please take another deep breath, stay present with your grief, and give it time to move through your body physically. And if you need to cry, allow yourself to release your pain.

Alex explained how being present with and containing her emotions felt like a superpower when she was in court. She recalled being on the stand with Tom's lawyer firing questions at her. She felt anxious and started to track her slight shakiness. Then she thought, "Okay, I am super anxious." She took some deep breaths, touched her feet to the ground, and stayed present with her anxiety. She then answered the lawyer's questions calmly and intelligently.

Lily also recently experienced the art of emotional self-regulation. In the throes of a heated conversation in which she was verbally abused, she (the inner witness) noticed her heart rate increasing, her teeth gritting, and her hands shaking. She felt fear and anger. Recognizing that her body's emotional response was normal and healthy, she took many deep breaths, remained calm, and respectfully asserted her boundaries. Shouting back in self-defense or getting angry would have thrown her body into a rage response and further provoked the other person. When the conversation ended, she didn't resort to her default tendencies of self-soothing with food or Netflix. Instead, she lit a candle and called a friend to talk and release the tension her body had held throughout the argument. Thus, emotional regulation doesn't mean you don't feel intensely; it simply means you don't allow your emotions to hijack your mind and behavior during or after the intense moment.

Emotional healing can occur when you are present with your emotions in an embodied way. When you can recognize and contain the bodily sensations of your emotion and its intentions, you are regulating your emotion—feeling without reacting. Understanding your emotion's purpose allows you to integrate the new information into the bigger picture of who you are. It feels liberating to experience your feelings without screaming or bottling them up.

Being present with and containing your feelings enables you to influence yourself! That is what empowerment means; you have power over yourself. Your feelings no longer control you, and you reclaim your emotional health. The emotional completion process gives you inner knowledge because you can stay present with intense, powerful emotions and learn from them. Embracing your feelings will help you recover from your TBR.

Reflection Questions: Experiencing and Containing Your Emotions

Practice this containing-your-emotions exercise at home.

1. Think of a time one of your emotions hijacked you, or you overreacted to a situation. Using your inner observer, describe what happened.

2. Can you name the emotion upon mindful reflection (inner observer)?

3. If you feel that emotion again (somatic mindfulness), notice your body's sensations and track them.

4. What is your emotion trying to communicate? What is its motive? Does it want you to set boundaries, confront someone, end a relationship, or protect yourself?

5. Next time you feel emotionally overwhelmed, go back to this practice to contain your emotions.

STOP COMPULSIVE THINKING

We have 6,000 thoughts a day, yikes![13] What we think affects how we feel. A TBR significantly impacts our thinking. Another trauma symptom from a TBR is intrusive overthinking or rumination. Rumination is when we are stuck in a mental loop of endless worries and problems. The thoughts come out of nowhere and seem impossible to control. The stream of excessive thoughts sounds like this: *How will I survive without him? Will I ever find love again? How do I return to a standard way of living? Will I get that job I need?* How *will my kids manage going back and forth between homes?* Usually, intrusive thoughts try to solve a worry about a future event or predict how something will happen. Yet, overthinking does the opposite; it makes us feel emotionally overwhelmed and causes anxiety.

This is where mindfulness comes in handy. You must use your mind to control your brain. When you catch yourself overthinking, hit the pause button and name what you are overthinking. It will help to divert your attention back to the present moment to stop rumination. An effective way to do so is through the grounding practice on page 159.

Also, rumination involves rethinking situations, analyzing them, and replaying them without forming an action plan or feeling a sense of resolution. Rumination is *not* problem-solving. So, it is best to transform useless overthinking into effective planning.

The acronym SMART (detailed below) will help you plan and strategize instead of lying in bed at night with thoughts pinging around. Your insomnia lessens when you stop overthinking because instead of staring at the ceiling, you can sleep knowing you have a plan.

SMART

Specific. The goal or plan is focused and concrete. You name the destination and decide how, when, and where to do it. For example, "I want to go back to school. I want to study social media design at . . ."

Measurable. Your goal can be described with a clear indicator of accomplishment. "I want to return to school to finish my bachelor's degree."

Achievable. The goal must be possible based on your resources, skills, and abilities. "I can do it; I just need to apply."

Realistic. Can you do something to accomplish your goal? "I can go to school in the evenings after work a few nights a week."

Time-limited. The goal has a set time when it can be implemented. A timeline is critical for focusing your plans. "I plan to apply to school by this January for entry in September."

Alex came into therapy exhausted; she had been up all night wondering how she would afford her life while paying her attorneys to fight Tom in court? I slowed her down and said, "Okay, let's pick a worry you can control." We decided when, where, and how to move to a new home. Although Tom was ordered to pay child support and alimony, Alex knew she could not afford to live in the house they owned. She decided to sell their home and find a rental (goal). She had to find somewhere nice but within budget (achievable). Alex knew she could afford a rental and planned the move (realistic). She gave herself a timeline of moving in three months (time-limited).

To stop scary thoughts from looping through your mind, devise a plan to address the problem you are worried about. That is productive thinking.

MANAGE INTRUSIVE EMOTIONAL FLASHBACKS

During your TBR, I am sure you remember feeling afraid because it is a natural response to feeling threatened. Emotional flashbacks are a typical C-PTSD symptom.[14] When your PL screams at you or throws a wine glass at you, fear is triggered to protect yourself and optimize your chance of survival. Living in an emotional war zone makes you hypervigilant because you want to mobilize to escape safely. The hyper-vigilance symptoms of anxiety, panic, and flashbacks still linger even after you have left your TBR. Let's unpack how to heal and recover from them.

Effective recovery requires practice to reduce your emotional flash-backs so you experience fewer negative emotions. When trapped in a flashback, you relive your TBR's worst emotional times. You know you are in a flashback when your emotional reactions are disproportional to your trigger. For example, a minor issue feels like an emergency, or a little glance from someone feels like they hate you. Or maybe you are alone and imagine your ex-PL gaining access to you and harming you. This is because the emotional memory part of your brain overrides your rational brain.

Actionable Steps for Managing an Emotional Flashback

1. **Bring in your inner observer:** Say, "I am having a flashback. I feel tiny, helpless, fearful, angry, or hopeless." Flashbacks make you feel like you are back in your TBR, surrounded by danger, yet your feelings and sensations are remnants from the past and cannot hurt you now.

2. **Soothe yourself:** "I feel afraid, but I am not in danger. I am safe here in the present moment." Remember, you are not living with your PL anymore. Take several slow deep breaths.

3. **Hold your boundaries:** You do not have to allow anyone to mistreat you. You can disconnect from any toxic person and stand up for yourself.

4. **Speak compassionately:** Create a short phrase you can say to yourself. "I am afraid right now, but things will work out for me." Refuse to shame, hate, or abandon yourself.

5. **Stop believing you will never heal:** During a trauma bond, fear and suffering felt endless—you thought you would always feel scared and helpless. Remind yourself, "That was then, and this is now. And now I am taking actionable steps to recover."

6. **Feel your body's fear without reacting:** Use your inner observer to track your physical sensations and take some calming breaths. Then go from feelings to facts: "I have left my PL"; "I no longer live with my PL"; or "I have a restraining order against my PL."

7. **Cocoon yourself:** Once you can find a place to calm down, wrap yourself in a weighted blanket (which is excellent for anxiety), make yourself a cup of tea, or take a hot bath. Allow yourself to cocoon so you can feel safe again.

If you have flashbacks regularly, I suggest you print out this list and put it in your bag or take a picture of it and have it on your phone. Just carrying an action plan will make you feel calmer. It is essential to recognize what triggers your emotional flashbacks. Initially, recognizing what things trigger you can be difficult because they happen unconsciously. Yet, over time, you will see a pattern, such as seeing someone who resembles your PL, experiencing anniversaries or birthdays, thinking someone is criticizing you, or believing someone is lying to you. Moreover, feeling tired, sick, or alone at home can trigger a flashback. Understanding what triggers you and having healthy flashback management will support recovery from being traumatized by your abusive, controlling ex-partner.

Intrusive Positive Flashbacks Caused by CD

Most people are familiar with negative flashbacks, yet a trauma symptom unique to TBRs is positive flashbacks. After you leave your traumatic attachment, you will be haunted by intrusive positive flashbacks.[15] You have two sets of conflicting CD memories: the intense, passionate love-bomber and the cruel, lying controller. The negative and positive memories compete for your brain's time. And as you try to recover from your TBR, you fear the positive flashbacks as much as the negative ones because the good memories eat away at the terrifying ones, making you crave your ex-abuser.

You get mad at yourself for longing for him because you fear returning to him. "What's wrong with me? This is crazy. I'm so stupid and weak for missing him after everything he's put me through," you think. Remember, flashbacks attack you and make you feel helpless. Also, these positive flashbacks compete with your thoughts of his psychopathic behavior. Reexperiencing the positive memories that come crashing in on you as you try to unglue yourself from your TBR is torturous. And it causes you to fear these unwanted positive memories.

However, please have compassion for yourself. Getting flooded by both sides of the relationship is expected.

Unfortunately, you get shamed by your friends, family, and even therapists for your low standards, codependency, love addiction, and fear of being alone. But it's your *trauma* symptom of intrusive positive flashbacks that can make you feel paralyzed. Even though you escaped your brain is trying to make sense of a confusing reality so you can make decisions and truly move on. Below are some ways in which you may experience positive flashbacks.

POSITIVE FLASHBACKS CAUSED BY COGNITIVE DISSONANCE

- Flashbacks of any positive event
- Replays from the early relationship (love-bombing), which create feelings of helplessness and fear of relapsing
- Positive memories that make you crave your ex PL
- Dreams about the events from the relationship, which create mixed feelings upon waking
- Avoiding people, places, and things that are reminders of positive experiences. Because the positive reminders trigger cognitive dissonance
- Strongly held positive memories that evoke positive feelings that interfere with remembering the toxic abuse and betrayal
- Intrusive, unrelenting thoughts of the positive and negative events mixed together in one memory[16]

To stop positive flashbacks, you first need to recognize what is happening to you. It is crucial to understand that you have intrusive positive memories. It makes sense that negative memories would haunt you, yet the atypical piece about a trauma bond is that the positive ones also traumatize you. After understanding that your positive memories are traumatic, you can connect them with the negative, traumatic ones. Linking the two types of memories allows you to view your ex-pathological partner consistently.[17] Your ex's good and bad sides were both abusive. His kindness was disingenuous, a behavior used in his recipe of intermittent abuse to control and manipulate you.

Instead of thinking of your PL as having two personalities with distinct behaviors, you must understand his actions as one person's continuous manipulation. Once you see both of his sides as *one pathological person*, your conflicting thoughts and feelings will subside because you have merged your lover's good and bad parts into one cohesive narrative.

To help reduce and eventually resolve your CD, you must replace the "he's good/he's bad" mindset, knowing that regardless of the side he displays, he is incapable of empathy and intimacy. In truth, your ex-partner is sadistic, calculating, controlling, and cruel. The love-bombing good side is as pathological as the abusive, controlling side. Once you link these two parts, your CD and fear of positive flashbacks will slowly reduce.[18]

Sandra L. Brown MA's research indicates that an effective way to manage your intrusive positive memories is to find an accountability person.[19] This can be a therapist, friend, or family member—someone to call when you are struggling and thinking, "If only I give him one more chance, I know he will change. On our anniversary, I remember he planned a romantic boat ride with champagne."

HEAL SHAME, HOPELESSNESS, AND DEPRESSION

Do you notice difficulty getting up in the morning and going to work? Or maybe you feel an inner emptiness and lack genuine pleasure. Perhaps you sleep and eat more or less than you would like to. Maybe you feel worn out, heavy-hearted, and weighed down. Ugh, you are experiencing depressive symptoms. Depression, a typical trauma symptom, causes you to lose faith in yourself and can interfere with your TBR recovery.

Shame, hopelessness, and depression cause so much misery for many women after their TBR. A TBR erodes your self-esteem and makes you feel insecure and ashamed. Shame and self-blame cause intense self-hatred and, unfortunately, are typical symptoms of C-PTSD.[20] Shame says you are flawed, unworthy, and broken. Yet you are not broken and in need of fixing; you have been deeply wounded by a pathological lover and require kindness, care, and support.

Hopelessness and depression tell you that even though you left your abuser, your life will never change, and you will never recover. Yet you have done the most challenging first step: leaving. So, yes, you can recover and grow.

Juno's relationship with Larry made her feel hopeless and despairing. And depression haunted her after her TBR. Week after week, she came to therapy and said, "I still feel so depressed, and I am forever tired." Juno was working as a schoolteacher, and her chronic back pain caused her to miss work due to frequent doctor's appointments. She expressed concern about possibly losing her job. Even though she was out of her TBR, she felt embarrassed and ashamed. She asked, "What is wrong with me that I can't get better?"

So many of my patients feel depressed and hopeless after leaving a TBR. But over time, Juno stopped her shaming thoughts and changed them to "Wow, Juno! Living with a controlling, abusive man who betrayed you must have been hard. It's okay to have moments when painful anguish consumes you." The tenderness she offered herself brought up her deep sadness, and she lay in her bed and had a deep, cleansing cry.

The benefits of self-compassion are many, and each stems from the same principle: how you talk to yourself affects how you think and feel. The goal of the practice is to be supportive, helpful, and compassionate toward yourself as you recover from your trauma bond. How self-compassionate are you? Check out the self-compassion scale on my website: https://drnae.com/self-compassion-scale.

Also, *fierce* self-compassion involves protecting and motivating yourself. The next time your PL threatens or intimidates you, think of yourself as a momma bear who ferociously protects her cubs. You can defend and motivate yourself to set boundaries, call your attorney, and provide yourself with what you need to thrive after leaving your trauma bond.

Offering self-compassion can initially feel awkward, especially since your PL was never remorseful or empathetic. And for women whose parents were emotionally, physically, or sexually abusive, fear is intermingled with signs of care. If you had to close the door on your heart to deal with early childhood pain, opening your heart unconditionally to yourself can remind you of your suffering and create a *backdraft*.[21] Now all your trapped suffering from your childhood and trauma bond come flying out. You want to close the door again and shut down your self-compassion. Yet this is a good sign because it means you are starting to take in your kindness and heal. So, if this happens, take a few calming breaths to stabilize and revisit your self-compassion practice later.

Self-compassionate people tend to be happier and more optimistic. Self-compassion feeds hope, and you need hope right now. Especially after a TBR, it's essential to go slowly and at your own pace. You can only learn new things if you feel safe, so please take responsibility for your safety, and only push yourself if it feels right. Be patient with yourself and use the guided self-compassion meditation I offer to support you in this new practice: https://drnae.com/meditations/self-compassion.

AVOIDING AVOIDANCE

Avoidance behaviors take many forms, including procrastinating, thinking about things rather than doing them, and being paralyzed by decision-making. In general, fear drives avoidance. Specifically fear of reality, failure, rejection, or anything that reminds us of pain.

Creating a life after leaving a relational prison causes anxiety and fear. So, avoiding life after a terrorizing experience is a normal response to trauma. But I am sure that you, like all adults, have an innate need to feel valuable, competent, and confident. Recovering from avoidance symptoms requires taking risks, facing your fears, and approaching life head-on.

It is hard to let go of avoidance, but the following skills and strategies can help you reduce it.

1. Replace avoidance with trying new things. Try to embrace life and its rewards rather than surviving it with as little pain and fear as possible.

2. Start by taking small steps. Break down each task into smaller, manageable steps—try to do each task a little at a time. Research shows that this way of approaching a goal works.[22]

3. Do something for its own sake rather than worrying whether you are doing it well enough. Avoidance is often caused by fear of not doing things perfectly or not being good enough. Instead of concentrating on the outcome, focus on the process.

4. Remember, getting better at things takes practice.

5. Anticipation is often more frightening than reality. Try things, and you will be surprised to see they often turn out better than expected.

6. The brain does not know the difference between imagination and reality. Imagine doing the desired task over and over again. See yourself doing it, then do it.

7. Have a good routine. Routines squash anxiety. Doing the same activities simultaneously and in the same place can help reduce avoidance.

Breaking free of avoidance is essential. Many new psychological studies show that persistence or grit, even more than intelligence or innate talent, is necessary to accomplish your goals.[23] Once you discover a personal calling toward a career, skill, or hobby, aim to become competent through repetition and dedication. This part includes taking the steps necessary to make these dreams a reality. It requires courage to take risks and approach what you fear. Where there is fear, there is transformation. Trust me: Once you face your fear and use your willpower and grit to accomplish a goal, you will feel delighted with yourself! Remember, fulfillment is an inside job.

Reflection Questions (Don't Avoid These!)

1. Do you have a pattern of avoiding people, tasks, or situations? Think of some examples.

2. What underlying fear or belief is soothed by avoidance?

3. When you think about avoiding, how does it feel? How does it feel immediately versus later? For instance, you may experience immediate relief by thinking about avoidance, helping you breathe easier. Then, when you process what happens after, you may feel anxiety and shame, which feels like a tightness in the chest and may make you hang your head.

4. What is a recent example of something or someone you avoided? Describe the situation, what feeling got soothed, and what fear you avoided.

5. What are the positive and negative consequences of your avoidance?

6. Describe an instance in which you pushed past your tendency to avoid and approach life. How did it make you feel to approach versus avoid something?

A critical thought to remember is that recovery is never linear; it's a dance of two steps forward and one step back. So please don't be hard on yourself when it feels like you are doing great and making progress, then suddenly you feel hopeless again. Symptoms are treatable and will improve with time. I am confident you will bounce forward after your TBR and become a surthriver; you will overcome suffering and flourish. And yes, you will live and love again! Maybe that's scary, maybe that's exciting—notice and be with whatever comes up for you.

KEY POINTS TO REMEMBER

1. Post-traumatic growth describes the emotional development you can experience after a trauma bond.

2. To begin recovery, you must practice consistent self-care to feel emotionally, physically, and mentally stable.

   • Mindful movement, like yoga, is an effective trauma-healing tool.

3. Mindfulness is a self-reflection skill allowing you to connect with your inner truth.

   • Mindfulness requires connecting with your inner witness to observe your thoughts and feelings.

   • Chronically retelling your TBR story can emotionally overwhelm and destabilize you. Share your TBR experiences only with trauma-informed therapists or support groups.

4. Learning the skill of setting boundaries will help you stop self-abandonment.

   • Take time to write your manifesto or relational rules to guide your boundaries.

5. Learning emotional containment teaches you how to be mindfully present with your emotions and understand their intentions.

6. Managing your emotional flashbacks requires using your inner observer.
   - Intrusive positive flashbacks are caused by cognitive dissonance.
   - To heal positive flashbacks, you must link negative and positive memories, allowing you to recognize the PL's actions as one continuous manipulation.

7. Practicing self-compassion heals depression, hopelessness, and shame.

8. Breaking free of avoidance is essential because persistence or grit, even more than intelligence or innate talent, is necessary to accomplish your goals.

9 Avoiding the Future PL

> The paradox of real love is that our capacity
> to sustain intimacy rests on our capacity
> to tolerate aloneness inside the relationship.[1]
>
> **−TERRENCE REAL**

DATING AGAIN AFTER ENDING YOUR TBR may be intimidating. It's okay to not be in a relationship for a while. Some experts say don't date for two years; some say a year. I suggest being kind to yourself and giving yourself at least a year before you enter back into dating. Your heart needs time to recover.

And I understand, after your hard work of relational detoxification, starting a new relationship can seem like climbing Mt. Everest. Opening up to a new person about who you are—your experiences, feelings, and memories—feels scary. You wonder, "How much do I tell them? Is this person trustworthy? Will my trauma bond experience scare them away?" Much like physical intimacy, emotional intimacy in a relationship is something many people feel they can engage in only with someone they trust. As a survivor, figuring out whether you can trust someone can be challenging. You thought you could trust your previous partner who turned out to be a toxic psychopath. You may have walls up no matter how nice a new person is.

It's okay—that's normal. The most important thing is to take things slowly. Trust has to be earned, not blindly given. If this new partner sticks around, they will not rush you to take down those walls. If they do, I'd consider that a red flag.

If you want to open up to your new partner but are afraid, try saying so honestly. If they respond with some version of "take your time, and I'm here to listen when you're ready," it's a good indicator that this person respects your boundaries. If they make fun of you or try to pressure you—"What's the big deal? Just tell me."—you know they're probably not going to be an ideal partner.

Disclosing abuse about your past can be retraumatizing. Not everyone deserves to hear your story, and you don't want to trauma dump on someone. Sharing your trauma shouldn't be an icebreaker topic but something you've carefully considered and decided on without outside pressure from others. Unlike when you were with the abusive partner, you are now in control of what you do and say—no one else.

However, this advice isn't one-size-fits-all. Lily told me, "I told men my baggage pretty quickly because if they ran the other way, then forget them." She wanted her dates to understand that she had been traumatized by a lover because she likes them to know how important it is that their words match their actions.

It's important to note that you are far stronger and more resilient than before your trauma bond. You have walked through fire and come out the other side. If men "run the other way," it is not a reflection of you, but rather them.

Just as talking about trauma can be triggering, hearing about it can be as well. That's why many people use the phrase "holding space" to describe when someone can listen to another person's past trauma. Not everyone is equipped to be nonjudgmental and compassionate. Yet, if sharing your TBR is what you need right now, request it. Lily's litmus test worked. She wanted to know right off the bat whether this was a deal-breaker, and for her new partner, it wasn't.

While honesty is a good foundation for building a healthy relationship, your safety is the top priority. Yet you may need to share your past relational trauma due to certain circumstances. You might live in a small town where everyone knows everyone or your previous and new partners might be acquaintances. Yet you get to choose how much and what exactly you will disclose.

What if you've already told your new lover about your past, and now, you're wondering if it was a good idea? What if your partner didn't support you after you disclosed? Or worse, what if they began using your past against you? Phrases like "You're just being paranoid because of your past" show that this new partner isn't respecting you. What if you've even started to see similarities in this partnership with your past abuser? This realization can be devastating, but don't blame yourself. You are not the reason someone else is an unsafe lover. But now you have a choice—stick it out and see if this person will change (did that work out for you with your PL?) or leave before you get in too deep.

Taking a step back is also okay if your gut "says no" when you are around your new love interest. You might want to consider checking in with someone else—your accountability partner or therapist—and get their opinion on the new mate. An outsider may see something you're blocking out because abusive tactics were once a "normal" part of your life.

I realize that trusting a lover again is terrifying. A list of red flags follows to remind you what to look for when dating.

1. Is he overconfident, a smooth talker, grandiose, or highly charismatic?

2. Does he want to move the relationship along quickly? After three weeks, does he say you're his soulmate?

3. Does he easily share his traumatized past?

4. Does he say his ex the craziest woman on the planet?

5. Does he call or text you more than five times daily?

6. Does he happen to have all the same interests as you?

7. Does he want to monopolize all your time?

8. Is there excessive alcohol or drug use?

9. Does he act jealous even though you have only gone on a few dates?

10. When you're with him, how does your gut feel? Trust your intuition.

11. Does he profess how much you can trust him? (Trustworthy guys don't always need to say that.)

12. Does he genuinely respect your boundaries? Not by what he says but by what he does.

HEALTHY CONNECTION

Unfortunately, as TBRs indicate, we live in a selfish patriarchal society, a culture that values capitalism, competition, and individuality. And in patriarchy, there is a hierarchy of one person being the top dog and one being the underdog. Patriarchy celebrates dominance, which entails having power over another.

Abuse of power and trust is at the root of traumatic bonding. Your pathological lover was on a power trip, and you were on a pleasing streak. Hence, after a TBR, you might need clarification about balancing being connected to others and not abandoning yourself. This section explains the concept of having your power and your partner having his while sharing intimacy.

In your TBR, your pathological lover felt superior and was grandiose. He felt he was above the civil rules you and I follow because he was better than us. He felt entitled to control you to meet his needs for power, pleasure, and money. Grandiosity might appear like healthy self-esteem, yet it is not.

The opposite is feeling shame—feeling inferior, less than others, and defective. Yet neither one of these is healthy self-esteem. Healthy self-esteem or self-worth is your capacity to value yourself, see yourself in a warm light, and know that everyone gets rejected, fails, and makes mistakes. Balanced self-esteem means you regard yourself as neither better nor worse than anyone else. Whether a person is Jeffrey Dahmer or Mother Teresa, they have equal essential value, worth, and dignity. Your worth is your birthright, yet you are treated as a worthless woman in a TBR.

The opposite of traumatic bonding is interdependent intimacy. It's natural to desire closeness and depend on your partner when you're in love. However, interdependent intimacy requires space, allowing lovers to be themselves. It requires the fundamental awareness that you are different from your partner yet connected. It includes both partners being equal and cherishing and valuing themselves and their lover without overpowering their partner or losing themselves.

Interdependent intimacy requires tolerating your partner's separateness and differences. It allows brutal honesty about your deepest desires, fears, needs, and feelings with the expectation of being heard. Nourishing communication requires a commitment to nonviolent living. Couples' expert Terry Real calls this "full respect living."[2] Like all the skills in this book, it requires practice. Before you shame or blame your partner, pause and ask, "Is what I am about to say respectful?" If it's not, don't say it. That rule also applies to your partner. Don't accept less than total respect, or you can end up in another TBR. In interdependent intimacy, neither partner is cruel and controlling or submissive and pleasing.

Alex described her first experience of dating after being in a trauma bond. She met Connor through mutual friends. They had a fantastic first blind date. He lived in the same town, had two young children, and loved playing pickleball. As nice as he was, Alex was freaked out about trusting another man again. She explained that after three months of dating, Alex felt like Connor was pushing things along too quickly (she did not want to be love-bombed again). One night eating sushi, she got the courage to tell him, "Connor, I am crazy for you, yet after my last relationship, I want to take things slowly." Connor responded, "Alex, I hear you, and that makes sense." Alex said that when she heard him say, "I hear you," she was shocked. Tom never said that to her. We ended her session with me saying to her, "Alex, if someone can't hear you, they can't love you."

Of course, all relationships have disagreements, but they should not leave one partner chronically frightened. Healthy disputes do not involve crazy-making fights that resolve nothing. A pathological lover never apologizes or takes accountability for causing pain because he does not feel empathy or remorse. When your behavior or words hurt your lover, it is essential to be accountable and say, "I am sorry I hurt you." When you feel wounded by your partner, you can use this nonviolent script from Terry Real:[3]

> This is what I remember happening.
> This is what I made up about it.
> This is what I felt.
> This is what I need or would help me feel better.

With healthy interdependence, both partners feel secure in themselves and the relationship. Only love based on honest self-expression between two equal partners can sustain healthy intimacy. Fiercely intimate lovers are compassionate toward each other. Their compassion is a choice; it does not come from a need to please or control. It comes from security rather than insecurity and genuine love rather than a need to control.

TIPS TO PREVENT TRAUMA BONDING

In addition to learning about and identifying the signs of a trauma bond, it is also helpful to learn tips that prevent you from entering a relationship of this type. As a start, I suggest the following:

1. Spend time knowing your wants, needs, and values.

2. Develop an awareness of your beliefs concerning love and relationships. What were your family of origin's messages about love? Do you agree with them? Or do you want to create your own beliefs and behaviors about loving?

3. Take your time moving into new relationships. Do not ignore any red flags; address them right away. And if your partner becomes volatile because you are trying to address an issue, do not ignore that information.

4. Create self-protection by setting boundaries from the start. Managing expectations is much easier when they are clearly stated and understood.

5. Learn healthy ways to self-soothe when you are upset. Develop a repertoire of self-soothing techniques to not get overwhelmed by your emotions.

6. Lower your tolerance for chaos in relationships and friendships. One of my favorite phrases has turned into my mantra: "I don't do dysfunctional relationships anymore."

KEY POINTS TO REMEMBER

1. When you decide to date after a TBR, keep in mind all the red flags to look for so you don't fall back into a trauma bond again.

2. Healthy connection involves you owning your power and your partner having his while sharing intimacy.

3. Interdependent intimacy requires full-respect living.

10 | Go Live

Willingness to experience aloneness,
I discover connection everywhere;
Turning to face my fear,
I meet the warrior who lives within.[1]

—JENNIFER WELWOOD,
EXCERPT FROM THE POEM "UNCONDITIONAL"

THE TORNADO OF A TBR leaves behind severe wreckage. It ruins families and women; destroys self-confidence, freedom, and personal growth; and causes humiliation, fear, economic ruin, heartbreak, physical harm, ugly custody battles, and decimated souls.

Yet, TBRs and abuse are avoidable and resolvable. This book explains how to spot and stop a TBR—now you know the how, who, what, and why so you can see them coming.

Pathological lovers have distorted your mind to control and exploit your heart. They specialize in creating mystery but withdrawing the curtain reveals someone without a moral compass who cannot love you. As I have explained, prioritizing your recovery is your immediate need after escaping your trauma vortex. I hope you now know love never warrants use and abuse. Emotional, mental, financial, and verbal abuse damages just like physical abuse. Love does not have to hurt or destroy you like before. Learning to live and love again means finding a balance: loving others without abandoning yourself.

My patients' number one fear is entering another TBR. Buying and reading this book confirms you are journeying away from loving a controlling, abusive man again. But reading is insufficient; learning takes effort and practice. Nobody can do it for you or save you—not your therapist, lawyer, coach, or friends. Yet, you desire to heal. No matter how depressed and isolated you have become or how devastating your TBR was, at your core exists a healing impulse. Imagine personal recovery work as an inner glow-up that will last a lifetime.

I know growth is uncomfortable. Yet, your innate desire to recover, combined with your new awareness and education, will support your recovery. Now you have a GPS and skills you can practice so you can return home to yourself and get back to living. Being a healthy adult requires not losing your authenticity while in love. After a TBR, getting your balance might seem impossible. However, personal growth occurs through awareness, commitment to you, and a willingness to try things differently.

By now, I hope you understand how to self-soothe, which has two parts: not losing yourself to the pressures and demands of others and developing your capacity to stabilize your emotions and fears. Your ability to maintain yourself while in love is the key to healthy intimacy. Taking the time to connect to your authenticity and being brave enough to live it will give you confidence. And for you to earn genuine self-esteem, you must put in the work and face your fears. You, my dear, are worth that effort.

Everyone talks about the difficulty of trusting people after being hurt. But hardly anyone shares the problem of trusting yourself after an abuser skillfully undermines your gut instincts and beliefs. I know that sentence resonated with you. Recovery is about putting the time and energy into learning to trust yourself to make healthy choices about whom to share intimacy with and knowing, when you meet a new lover, how to discern whether he sees you as an object to use and exploit or a unique person to cherish, respect, and treat tenderly.

Anyone with an education and a kind heart can help sweep our society clean of TBRs. We all have a stake in ending abuse for ourselves and our children. TBRs are the product of a culture that excuses and condones bullying and exploiting others for selfish reasons. It promotes narcissism and blames the abused.

Your recovery is demanding enough, so it is not your job to help other women unless you decide to. Yet, if you want societal norms to change, you must let people know you have the right to live free of abuse, control, insults, domination, manipulation, and exploitation. Moreover, you must stand up to people trying to take your rights. Living free of trauma bonds will inspire others to do so.

Encourage women in your life to own their power and insist on dignity and respect from others. Meanwhile, expect people to be kind and respectful and don't accept anything less. Lastly, if someone has hurt you and can't own it, they can't change. "Accountability is a MUST" is your new mantra.

On that note, don't expect accountability or closure from your ex-lover. Getting closure from him is overrated. The only apology you need is the one you owe yourself for staying as long as you did. The only person you need to have a conversation with, and the only person you need to see again, is the person in the mirror. Look at yourself and say, "You know what? I fell for an abusive con artist. It happens to people everywhere. Yet, I know I am worthy of healthy intimacy. I am a surthriver." That's your closure. Don't keep trying to get the devil to feel remorse and wonder why you're still in hell.

We have been fed a myth of romantic love that we must debunk. Intimacy is not about one person having the power to save and care for their lover. True intimacy involves tenderness and being kind to the one you love while also holding space for them to be the unique individual they are. It requires a person who loves you and cannot bear to see you suffer, so their intention is to make your life easier and not a source of torture. And love requires the courage to reveal who you are by letting yourself be known. When a partner says he will change, please remember to tell him, "I am in the show-me phase, not the tell-me phase." A lover's words must match his actions.

Healing is a messy journey. Occasionally, you will feel yourself skidding back and losing your balance again. All the old patterns and crazy feelings may come rushing in. All the self-doubt and fear may make you want to hide. It's normal and okay. You can pick yourself up again and get through it. Call your therapist, call a friend, and be patient and tender with yourself. Restart and keep doing the little things you have learned and know how to do. You have survived a trauma bond; you can do anything.

Writing this last section, I feel tears in my eyes and a fullness in my heart. With you in mind, I have dedicated my life to writing this book for the past two years. No therapist or psychological theory can take away life's inevitable pain. You can learn how to develop a tolerance for life—with a greater capacity to feel and self-soothe so you can live and love peacefully. I hope you will develop the strength and wisdom to love and be loved well, knowing that one day you will truly feel humbly inviolable (never broken again).

Acknowledgments

WHEN I EXPERIENCED MY TRAUMA BOND thirty years ago, there was little information about pathological love relationships and narcissism. Thank goddesses, that's changed. My work comes from a lifetime of experience and professional research. I am beyond grateful to stand on the shoulders of giants who have highlighted trauma, specifically relational trauma between lovers. There are too many authors and researchers to thank. I will name those whose work has impacted my learning the most. First, Hervey Cleckly's book *The Mask of Sanity* is foundational. It illustrates how the psychopath who lives among us wears a mask that conceals his mental disorder. Robert Hare clarified Cleckley's work in 1970 with the Psychopathy Checklist.

Edward Gondolf's research on battered women as survivors further enlightened me about the resilient nature of abused women. Psychologist Donald G. Dutton's work, research, and writings in 1990 painted a dramatic and informative portrait of the man who harms his intimate partner. And Michael P. Johnson, who differentiated the two types of intimate partner violence into situational couples violence and intimate terrorism, added a deeper aspect to the research.

Next, Lundy Bancroft studied and researched the pathological lover. This author taught the world the whys and hows of the violent partner's motivations and controlling behaviors. Over the past five years, I have read all the research of Joshua D. Miller, Don Lyman, and Keith Miller, the rock star researchers of the Dark Tetrad. Meanwhile, trauma experts Dr. Laurence Heller, Dr. Aline La Pierre, and Dr. Arielle Schwartz helped me develop a map for healing from trauma bonds.

However, no theorist's work has influenced me as much as that of therapist Sandra L. Brown, MA. In 2018, I was rocked when I read Brown's seminal book *Women Who Love Psychopaths*. Two decades after I left my ex-husband, her words, teaching, and scholarly education identified that which I always knew inside: I was not responsible for the abuse I endured. Brown's research into how personality traits can make a woman a victim of a Dark Tetrad lover has been proven. Through her research, she further defined the pathological lover's personality. I am forever grateful to Brown for her research—it shapes my daily work with my patients.

Writing this book was one of the hardest things I have ever done. So many people helped and inspired me. Let's start at the beginning. As a therapist, woman, and mother, I genuinely appreciate the value of *my* mother's love; I was very blessed. Mom, every word I wrote on every page is because I am your daughter. You died over twenty years ago, yet your effect on my life has been profound. Suzanne, I am your daughter. I am bringing this work to the public because you taught me the value of understanding myself every night at the dinner table. Conversations with you were like a drug; therefore, I became a therapist.

To my husband, John: Your dedication to my love taught me that love is messy and imperfect but doesn't have to be traumatic. Our love was not traumatic because of your willingness to change and grow. I love you, John. Your desire to love me helped me this past year when I did not believe I could finish this book. Our passion has also inspired many of these pages, and I would not have it any other way. Indeed, our love forced me to grow, too.

And to my angels, Chandler, Carter, Nikkie, and Allie, my loves, my children: I have suffered a lot, and I would do it all again to share our beautiful parent-child relationship. Channy and Carter, you were meant to be my children; you are the greatest gifts of my life.

Clara: We met at the right time—another example of the power of relationships. Your belief in me and your tremendous support with editing made this book a reality. Your dedication to healing from your numerous trauma bonds is beyond inspirational, and your words are imbued through the pages.

David Endris: Thank you so much for believing in me and offering to publish my book. And dear Erin, my writing fairy: You brought my words to life so the reader can learn and grow. I am grateful for your dedication to getting this manuscript to fruition.

To my beautiful, brave patients: You are my daily inspiration. As I wrote these pages, you were always on my mind. How can I help you heal from the pain of trauma bonds? And to the women I have never met: I am so sorry you have endured such pain from a lover. Yet I know you can and will heal. I have given up two years of my life for women everywhere because you are all worth it.

Love, Dr. Nae

Resources

DOMESTIC VIOLENCE 24-HOUR HOTLINES TO CALL OR TEXT

National Domestic Violence Hotline

This resource provides confidential, nonpublic, one-on-one chats with advocates. The hotline is available 24/7/365 in both English and Spanish at 1-800-799-7233.

Live Violence Free Crisis Line: 530-544-4444

US Domestic Violence Text Line: Text "START" to 88788. For more information, go to https://www.thehotline.org/.

911 Tip

If you cannot speak to the operator in an emergency, dial 911 and place your phone in your pocket or nearby. Talk to your abuser in a way that communicates to the operator that you are in danger. Use statements such as "Please stop! I'm scared for my life. Don't hurt me!" The operator will automatically dispatch someone to your location.

MOBILE APPS FOR VICTIMS AND SURVIVORS

eBodyGuard

eBodyGuard is a voice- or button-activated app that notifies a pre-designated emergency contact and US-based 911 responders of your emergency and location. It records audio that can be used as evidence in a criminal investigation.

eBodyGuard is an information system–compliant app, making the data more admissible in court. The FBI certified the data collection process and the eBodyGuard team to collect and record crime scene data.

TapeACall Pro

Because threats and protection order violations often occur over the phone, it's worth recording phone conversations with your abuser. TapeACall allows you to record incoming/outgoing phone calls without indicating to the other party that they're being recorded. Recording and retrieving audio files are simple.

Noonlight

Feel more secure traversing uncomfortable locations and situations. Hold a button on your phone's screen when you feel unsafe. If the button is released, 911 is contacted, and police are dispatched. To cancel the call, enter your four-digit PIN. This app is intuitive and straightforward.

myPlan

This free app helps assess a partner's danger level. Answer a series of questions for yourself or someone else to receive a danger score on a scale from 0 to 20, followed by an action plan to help determine the next steps. Easy and quick to use, it provides 24/7 advocate support through an embedded live chat feature.

RUSafe

Based on a highly regarded danger assessment tool, this free assessment and journaling app helps individuals decide if they are in a dangerous situation with a potential abuser. It's free to download, works with iPhone and Android phones, and includes a secure journal feature where text, audio, and photos can be uploaded and sent to your email.

Aspire

Your trusted contacts receive an SOS text or voice message when you need help. Created by the When Georgia Smiled: Robin McGraw Revelation Foundation, this app is disguised as a news feed, a super-smart feature considering abusive partners often monitor victims' phone activity. It is hidden well so that an abuser may be none the wiser.

Talking Parents

This app provides co-parents with a secure, accountable, and complete record of all communication. It includes payments, calling, messaging, planning, and coordination tools for organized co-parenting. It records all easily accessed conversations that could be admissible in court.

OurFamilyWizard

This app helps you solve shared custody challenges faster, without confusion, and with less conflict. It's a powerful tool to help you document parenting time, reimbursement requests, payments, exchanges, and more.

Pro: keeps track of emails sent, read, and replied to.

DOMESTIC VIOLENCE ONLINE SUPPORT

Suppose you want to connect through chat rooms with other domestic violence and sexual assault survivors, advocates, or therapists. If so, this list of online resources—including message boards, forums, social media groups, and telehealth hotlines—will help. If you join an online conversation, please remember not to use your real name or contact information and only use a safe email address if required. You never know who else may see your posts. Also, practice safe surfing so your online activity stays confidential.

AfterSilence.org

AfterSilence aims to help victims become survivors and communicate in recovering from domestic and sexual violence. It offers an active message board and chat room for rape, sexual assault, sexual abuse, incest, and molestation survivors. There are over 31,000 members and about one million posts, including recent posts and many helpful posts from days and months past.

DomesticShelters.org Facebook Group

One of the most active places where domestic violence victims and survivors converse is this website's Facebook page. There is a daily conversation, with people sharing opinions, past experiences, and real stories, and occasional advice from professionals who have joined in on a topic, all within the context of an archive of articles on a wide range of domestic violence topics.

Speak Your Truth Today

Speak Your Truth Today (SYTT) was sparked when one woman opened up about the story of her abusive marriage on Facebook. She posted on her twenty-fourth birthday to bring awareness to domestic violence against women—however, as it grew more popular, men who suffered domestic violence and adults who suffered child abuse also came forward, sharing their stories. So, on a whim, she made a Facebook group for all domestic violence victims and survivors, hoping they could share encouragement and resources with those recovering from abuse. SYTT has now become a massive community, with over 18,000 members from all over the world.

Fort Refuge

This clever grassroots site is run by survivors for fellow survivors as a safe place to come together and discuss their struggles and victories when healing from various types of abuse. Though the forum and chat do not boast the same numbers as some larger organizations, they are still currently some of the more active online forums. Fort Refuge also adds new content to its site regularly.

Love Is Respect—National Teen Dating Helpline

As its name suggests, this resource focuses on teen relationships. It is accessible by phone, text, or live chat. Run by the National Domestic Violence Hotline, it offers real-time, one-on-one support from trained peer advocates who provide information and advocacy to those involved in abusive dating relationships. It also works with concerned parents, teachers, clergy, law enforcement, and service providers.

Pandora's Aquarium

Pandora's Aquarium is an online forum with around two million posts and over 70,000 members run by Pandora's Project. It provides information, support, and resources to rape and sexual abuse survivors and their friends and family. These resources include healing retreat weekends, an articles database, and guest speaker chats.

Out of the Fog

This organization helps family members and loved ones of people who have personality disorders.

Aftermath: Surviving Psychopathy

The Aftermath: Surviving Psychopathy Foundation is dedicated to educating the public about the nature of psychopathy and its cost to individuals and society. It seeks to support the families and victims of those with psychopathy.

The Institute for Relational Harm Reduction

Safe Relationships Magazine provides a place for survivors and treatment providers to access pathology information and recovery services to assist in understanding Cluster B personality disorders and pathological love relationships.

BOOKS

Why Does He Do That? Inside the Minds of Angry and Controlling Men
by Lundy Bancroft
This book answers the twenty questions women commonly ask about controlling or abusive relationship partners. These questions include why an abusive partner treats other people better than he treats you, how he came to be the way he is, why his good periods don't last, and how to tell if he will change.

Getting Free: You Can End Abuse and Take Back Your Life
by Ginny NiCarthy
This book is a supportive, clear, and convenient guide to understanding if your partner is abusive and what steps to take to get your life back under your control. Everything is here, from stopping blaming yourself to choosing a good counselor or lawyer. I give this book my highest recommendation.

When Love Goes Wrong: What to Do When You Can't Do Anything Right
by Ann Jones and Susan Schechter
This powerful book is for women who are seeking guidance on how to cope with a controlling partner and how to move toward freedom and recovery. It is practical, down-to-earth, and accurate, and it covers in detail a wide range of issues that women face. It is a wonderful resource.

It's My Life Now: Starting Over After an Abusive
Relationship or Domestic Violence
by Meg Kennedy Dugan and Roger Hock
Despite the title, this book is as equally valuable for women still involved with an angry or controlling partner as for those who have left. It is a beautiful, warm, compassionate book by authors who deeply understand emotional and physical abuse.

The Verbally Abusive Relationship: How to Recognize It
and How to Respond
by Patricia Evans
Evans's book takes the reader through the details of verbally abusive tactics people use in relationships and how to understand their effects on you. She offers terrific insights and practical advice. (The book contains a few common misconceptions about the psychology of abusers, but this is a minor drawback compared to its many strengths.)

Into the Light: A Guide for Battered Women
by Leslie Cantrelli
This booklet is short and straightforward, with accurate information and sound advice. It is an excellent resource for women with neither the time nor energy for the longer books listed here or who want some quick inspiration handy.

Not to People Like Us: Hidden Abuse in Upscale Marriages
by Susan Weitzman
This is a valuable exposé of abuse among the wealthy and includes essential guidance for abused women. Weitzman's descriptions of abusive men are accurate and helpful, but some myths slip in. I recommend this book highly.

Insight is 20/20: How to Trust Yourself to Protect Yourself from Narcissistic Abuse & Toxic Relationships
by Chelli Pumphrey
Chelli Pumphrey's anecdotes, clinical examples, and research teach you about body signals that can alert you to the dangers of a pathological partner. You'll learn to prevent, identify, or leave abusive or toxic relationships.

Why Can't I Leave? A Guide to Waking Up and Walking
By Kristen Milstead
"Kristen Milstead provides a social psychological analysis of narcissistic abuse using the empathetic voice of a survivor. Survivors who read this book will be able to trust the 'lightbulb' moments this rare perspective offers."—Bree Bonchay, LCSW, founder of World Narcissistic Abuse Awareness Day (WNAAD)

Character Disturbance: The Phenomenon of Our Age
by George Simon
Modern permissiveness and the new culture of entitlement allow disturbed people to reach adulthood without proper socialization. In a book for the general public and professionals, bestselling author and psychologist George Simon plainly explains how most disturbed characters think and behave.

Women Who Love Psychopaths: Inside the Relationships of Inevitable Harm with Psychopaths, Sociopaths & Narcissists
by Sandra L. Brown, MA
Learn the signs and symptoms of life- and soul-destroying disorders— and the impact on the partner, children, and societal systems—before you end up in one of these relationships of "inevitable harm," and why everyone should be concerned.

The Complex PTSD Workbook: A Mind-Body Approach to Regaining Emotional Control & Becoming Whole
by Arielle Schwartz
In *The Complex PTSD Workbook*, you'll learn about C-PTSD and gain valuable insight into the symptoms associated with unresolved childhood trauma. Take healing into your own hands while applying strategies to help integrate positive beliefs and behaviors.

Trauma and Recovery: The Aftermath of Violence—From Domestic Abuse to Political Terror
by Judith Herman, MD
Trauma and Recovery is a seminal text on understanding trauma survivors. By placing individual experience in a broader political frame, Harvard psychiatrist Judith Herman argues that psychological trauma is inseparable from its social and political context. Drawing on her research on incest and the vast literature on combat veterans and victims of political terror, she shows surprising parallels between personal horrors such as child abuse and public horrors such as war.

Notes

PREFACE

1. Lundy Bancroft, *Why Does He Do That? Inside the Minds of Angry and Controlling Men* (Penguin Random House, 2002): 19.

INTRODUCTION: THE PARADOX OF LOVE

1. Sigmund Freud, *Civilization and Its Discontents* (Internationaler Psychoanalytischer Verlag Wien, 1930).

2. N. Z. Hilton, *Domestic Violence Risk Assessment: Tools for Effective Prediction and Management, 2nd Edition* (American Psychological Association, 2021): 1.

3. Laurence Heller and Brad J. Kammer, *The Practical Guide for Healing Developmental Trauma Using the Neuroaffective Relational Model to Address Adverse Childhood Experiences and Resolve Complex Trauma* (North Atlantic Books, 2022).

4. Patrick J. Carnes, *The Betrayal Bond: Breaking Free of Exploitive Relationships, revised ed.* (Health Communications Inc., 2019).

5. Richard G. Tedeschi and Lawrence Calhoun, "The Posttraumatic Growth Inventory: Measuring the Positive Legacy of Trauma," *Journal of Trauma Stress* 9 (1996): 455–471, https://doi.org/10.1007/BF02103658.

CHAPTER 1: WHAT YOUR MOTHER NEVER TOLD YOU

1. Patrick J. Carnes, *The Betrayal Bond: Breaking Free of Exploitive Relationships, revised ed.* (Health Communications Inc., 2019).

2. Erich Fromm, *The Art of Loving* (Harper & Row, 1956).

3. Carnes, *The Betrayal Bond*.

4. Alex R. Piquero et al., "Domestic Violence During the COVID-19 Pandemic—Evidence from a Systematic Review and Meta-Analysis," *Journal of Criminal Justice* 74 (2021), https://doi.org/10.1016/j. jcrimjus.2021.101806.

5. Martin R. Huecker et al., "Domestic Violence," National Library of Medicine (Stat Pearls Publishing, 2022).

6. Huecker et al., "Domestic Violence."

7. Yuji Kanemasa, Yuki Miyagawa, and Takashi Arai, "Do the Dark Triad and Psychological, Intimate Partner Violence Mutually Reinforce Each Other? An Examination from a Four-Wave Longitudinal Study," *Personality and Individual Differences* (2022): 196, https://doi. org/10.1016/j.paid.2022.111714.

8. Gayle Brewer et al., "Dark Triad Traits and Romantic Relationship Attachment, Accommodation, and Control," *Personality and Individual Differences* 120 (2018): 202–208, https://doi.org/10.1016/j. paid.2017.09.008.

9. Lisa A. Fontes, *Invisible Chains: Overcoming Coercive Control in Your Intimate Relationship* (The Guilford Press, 2015).

10. Susan Painter and Donald Dutton, "Patterns of Emotional Bonding in Battered Women: Traumatic Bonding," *International Journal of Women's Studies* 8 (1970): 363–375, https://psycnet.apa.org/ record/1987-07585-001.

11. Jeffry A. Simpson et al., "Power and Social Influence in Relationships," in M. Mikulincer et al., eds., *APA Handbook of Personality and Social Psychology* 3 (American Psychological Association, 2015): 393–420, https://doi.org/10.1037/14344-015.

12. Painter and Dutton, "Patterns of Emotional Bonding."

13. Donald G. Dutton, *The Abusive Personality: Violence and Control in Intimate Relationships* (The Guilford Press, 2007).

CHAPTER 2: IS HE TWISTED OR TENDER?

1. Peter Trachtenberg, *The Casanova Complex: Compulsive Lovers and Their Women* (Eden, 1989).

2. Daniel J. Fox, *Antisocial, Narcissistic, and Borderline Personality Disorders: A New Conceptualization of Development, Reinforcement, Expression, and Treatment* (Routledge, 2020).

3. Lundy Bancroft, *Why Does He Do That? Inside the Minds of Angry and Controlling Men* (Penguin Random House, 2002).

4. Sandra L. Brown, MA, *Women Who Love Psychopaths: Inside the Relationships of Inevitable Harm with Psychopaths, Sociopaths & Narcissists* (Mask Publishing, 2018).

5. Thomas A. Widiger and Paul T. Costa Jr., eds., *Personality Disorders and the Five-Factor Model of Personality, Third Edition* (American Psychological Association, 2013), http://www.jstor.org/stable/j.ctv1chs8rh.

6. Felicity Morris, dir., Bernadette Higgins, prod., *Tinder Swindler*, Raw TV, 2022, Netflix.

7. Michael L. Crowe et al., "Exploring the Structure of Narcissism: Toward an Integrated Solution," *Journal of Personality Assessment* (2019), https://doi.org/: 10.1111/jopy.12464.

8. C. E. Sleep et al., "Uncovering the Structure of Antagonism," *Personality Disorders: Theory, Research, and Treatment* 12(4) (2021): 300–311, https://doi.org/10.1111/jopy.12464.

9. B. Fehr, D. Samson, and D. L. Paulhus, "The Construct of Machiavellianism: Twenty Years Later," in C. D. Spielberger and J. N. Butcher, eds., *Advances in Personality Assessment* 9 (1992): 77–116.

10. Brown, MA, *Women Who Love Psychopaths*.

11. Fox, *Antisocial, Narcissistic, and Borderline Personality Disorders*.

12. Hervey Milton Cleckley, *The Mask of Sanity: An Attempt to Reinterpret the So-Called Psychopathic Personality* (Mosby, 1941).

13. Stephen D. Hart, Robert D. Hare, and Timothy J. Harpur, "The Psychopathy Checklist—Revised (PCL–R), an Overview for Researchers and Clinicians," in J. C. Rosen and P. McReynolds, eds., *Advances in Psychological Assessment* 8 (1985): 103–130, https://doi.org/10.1007/978-1-4757-9101-3_4.

14. William McCord and Joan McCord, *Psychopathy and Delinquency* (Grune & Stratton Inc., 1956).

15. Reid Meloy, *Violent Attachments* (Jason Aronson Inc., 1992).

16. Robert D. Hare, "Psychopathy as a Risk Factor for Violence," *Psychiatric Quarterly* 70 (1999): 181–197, https://doi.org/10.1023/A:1022094925150.

17. Reece Akhtar, Gorkan Ahmetoglu, and Tomas Chamorro-Premuzic,

"Greed Is Good? Assessing the Relationship Between Entrepreneurship and Subclinical Psychopathy," *Personality and Individual Differences* 54(3) (2013): 420–425, https://doi.org/10.1016/j.paid.2012.10.013.

18. Robert D. Hare, *Without Conscience: The Disturbing World of the Psychopaths Among Us* (Pocket Books, 1993).

19. Adam C. Davis et al., "Longitudinal Associations Between Primary and Secondary Psychopathic Traits, Delinquency, and Current Dating Status in Adolescence," *Evolutionary Psychology* (2022), https://journals.sagepub.com/doi/10.1177/14747049211068670.

20. Bruno Bonfá-Araujo et al., "Considering Sadism in the Shadow of the Dark Triad Traits: A Meta-Analytic Review of the Dark Tetrad," *Personality and Individual Differences* (2022): 197, https://doi.org/10.1016/j.paid.2022.111767.

21. Gayle Brewer and Loren Abell, "Machiavellianism and Sexual Behavior: Motivations, Deception, and Infidelity," *Personality and Individual Differences* 74 (2014), https://doi.org/10.1016/j.paid.2014.10.028.

22. *Tell Me Lies*, episodes 1-18, Hulu, 2022.

23. Richard von Krafft-Ebing, *Psychopathia Sexualis* (Arcade Publishing, 2011), https://www.perlego.com/book/957137/psychopathia-sexualis-the-classic-study-of-deviant-sex-pdf.

24. Donald G. Dutton, *The Abusive Personality: Violence and Control in Intimate Relationships* (The Guilford Press, 2007).

25. Brown, MA, *Women Who Love Psychopaths*.

26. Satoru Kiire, Noboru Matsumoto, and Eri Yoshida, "Discrimination of Dark Triad Traits Using the UPPS-P Model of Impulsivity," *Personality and Individual Differences* 167 (2020), https://doi.org/10.1016/j.paid.2020.110256.

27. Barış Sevi, Betul Urgancy, and Ezgi Sakman, "Who Cheats? An Examination of Light and Dark Personality Traits as Predictors of Infidelity," *Personality* and *Individual Differences* 164 (2020), https://doi.org/10.1016/j.paid.2020.110126.

CHAPTER 3: TRAUMA BONDING

1. Sandra L. Brown, MA, *Women Who Love Psychopaths: Inside the Relationships of Inevitable Harm With Psychopaths, Sociopaths & Narcissists* (Mask Publishing, 2018).

2. Jordan G. Gibby and Jason B. Whiting, "Insecurity, Control, and Abuse: What Attachment Theory Can Teach Us About Treating Intimate Partner Violence," *Contemporary Family Therapy* 47 (2023), https://doi.org/10.1007/s10591-021-09623-4.

3. Brown, MA, *Women Who Love Psychopaths*.

4. Carl G. Jung, *Two Essays on Analytical Psychology* (London, 1953), 190.

5. Dale Archer, "The Manipulative Partner's Most Devious Tactic," *Psychology Today* (2017).

6. Brown, MA, *Women Who Love Psychopaths*.

7. Anthony W. Bateman, FRCPsych, and Peter Fonagy, eds., *Handbook of Mentalizing in Mental Health Practice, 2nd Edition* (American Psychiatric Association, 2019).

8. David Schnarch, *Passionate Marriage* (W. W. Norton & Company, 2009).

9. Vesna Gojković, Jelena Dostanić, and Veljko Đurić, "Structure of Darkness: The Dark Triad, the 'Dark' Empathy, and the 'Dark' Narcissism." *Primenjena psihologija* 15 (2022): 237–268, https://doi.org/10.19090/pp.v15i2.2380.

10. David Schnarch, *Brain Talk: How Mind Mapping Brain Science Can Change Your Life and Everyone in It* (Sterling Publishers, 2018).

11. A. H. Modell, *Imagination and the Meaningful Brain* (MIT Press, 2003).

12. O. Gilbar, C. Taft, and R. Dekel, "Male Intimate Partner Violence: Examining the Roles of Childhood Trauma, PTSD Symptoms, and Dominance," *Journal of Family Psychology* 34 (2020), 1004–1013, https://doi.org/10.1037/fam0000669.

13. Bojana M. Dinić and Anja Wertag, "Effects of Dark Triad and HEXACO Traits on Reactive/Proactive Aggression: Exploring the Gender Differences," *Personality and Individual Differences* 123 (2018): 44–49, https://doi.org/10.1016/j.paid.2017.11.003.

14. Michael P. Johnson, *A Typology of Domestic Violence: Intimate Terrorism, Violent Resistance, and Situational Couple Violence* (Boston: Northeastern University, 2008).

15. Oxford University Press, 2023, languages.oup.com.

16. Ekin Ok et al., "Signaling Virtuous Victimhood as Indicators of Dark Triad Personalities," *Journal of Personality and Social Psychology* 120(6) (2021): 1634–1661, https://doi.org/10.1037/pspp0000329.

17. Lisa A. Fontes, *Invisible Chains: Overcoming Coercive Control in Your Intimate Relationship* (The Guilford Press, 2015).

18. C. E. Sleep et al., "Uncovering the Structure of Antagonism," *Personality Disorders: Theory, Research, and Treatment* 12(4) (2021), https://doi.org/10.1037/per0000416.

19. Martha Stout, *Outsmarting the Sociopath Next Door: How to Protect Yourself Against a Ruthless Manipulator* (Harmony Books, 2020).

20. DomesticShelters.org.

21. Domina Petric, *Gaslighting and the Knot Theory of Mind* (2018), https://doi.org/10.13140/RG.2.2.30838.86082.

22. Barış Sevi, Betul Urgancy, and Ezgi Sakman, "Who Cheats? An Examination of Light and Dark Personality Traits as Predictors of Infidelity," *Personality and Individual Differences* 164 (2020), https://doi.org/10.1016/j.paid.2020.110126.

CHAPTER 4: OPPOSITES DO ATTRACT

1. Kai-Lilly Karpman, "Dusk Rises," in *No More Trauma Bonding: A Therapist's Guide to Healing from Traumatic Love.*

2. Melody Beattie, *Codependent No More: How to Stop Controlling Others and Start Caring for Yourself* (Harper Collins Publisher, 1987).

3. Sandra L. Brown, MA, and Jennifer R. Young, LMHC, "Five-Factor Form/Five-Factor Model Rating Form Traits of Agreeableness and Conscientiousness in Pathological Love Relationship Dynamics, An Interagency Report," *The Institute's Therapist Training Program and Manual: Treating the Aftermath of Pathological Love Relationships* (2014).

4. C. Robert Cloniger, *The Temperament and Character Inventory (TCI): A Guide to Its Development and Use* (St. Louis, Missouri: Center for Psychobiology of Personality, 1994), https://www.worldcat.org/title/temperment-and-characterter-inventory-tci-a-guide-to-its-development-and-use/oclc/32133789.

5. Thomas A. Widiger and Paul T. Costa Jr., eds., *Personality Disorders and the Five-Factor Model of Personality, Third Edition* (American Psychological Association, 2013), http://www.jstor.org/stable/j.ctv1chs8rh.

6. Sandra L. Brown, MA, *Women Who Love Psychopaths: Inside the Relationships of Inevitable Harm with Psychopaths, Sociopaths & Narcissists* (Mask Publishing, 2018).

7. Brown, MA, *Women Who Love Psychopaths.*

8. Sandra L. Brown, MA, Institute for Relational Harm Online Training, 2023, http://survivortreatment.com/.

9. Brown, MA, *Women Who Love Psychopaths.*

10. Widiger and Costa, eds., *Personality Disorders.*

11. Laurence Heller and Brad J. Kammer, *The Practical Guide for Healing Developmental Trauma Using the Neuroaffective Relational Model to Address Adverse Childhood Experiences and Resolve Complex Trauma* (North Atlantic Books, 2022).

12. Michael P. Johnson, *A Typology of Domestic Violence: Intimate Terrorism, Violent Resistance, and Situational Couple Violence* (Boston: Northeastern University, 2008).

13. Gerda Lerner, *The Creation of Patriarchy* (Oxford University Press, 1986).

14. Judith Herman, *Trauma and Recovery: The Aftermath of Violence from Domestic Abuse to Political Terror* (Basic Books, 1992).

15. Sander Thomaes et al., "Turning Shame Inside-Out: 'Humiliated Fury' in Young Adolescents," *Emotion* 11(4) (2011): 786–93, https://psycnet.apa.org/record/2011-10738-001.

CHAPTER 5: EMOTIONAL SCAR TISSUE

1. Patrick J. Carnes, *The Betrayal Bond: Breaking Free of Exploitive Relationships, revised ed.* (Health Communications Inc., 2019).

2. Martin Seligman, "Depression and Learned Helplessness," in R. J. Friedman, M. M. Katz, eds., *The Psychology of Depression: Contemporary Theory and Research* (New York: Winston-Wiley, 1974): 83–113.

3. E. W. Gondolf, *Battered Women as Survivors: An Alternative to Treating Learned Helplessness* (New York: Lexington Books, 1988).

4. Sandra L. Brown, MA, Institute for Relational Harm Online Training, 2023, http://survivortreatment.com/.

5. Laurence Heller and Brad J. Kammer, *The Practical Guide for Healing Developmental Trauma Using the Neuroaffective Relational Model to Address Adverse Childhood Experiences and Resolve Complex Trauma* (North Atlantic Books, 2022).

6. Lundy Bancroft, *Why Does He Do That? Inside the Minds of Angry and Controlling Men* (Penguin Random House, 2002).

7. Brown, MA, training session.

8. Sandra L. Brown, MA, *Women Who Love Psychopaths: Inside the Relationships of Inevitable Harm With Psychopaths, Sociopaths & Narcissists* (Mask Publishing, 2018).

9. Brown, MA, training session.

10. Brown, MA, training session.

11. Brown, MA, *Women Who Love Psychopaths*.

12. Brown, MA, training session.

13. Arielle Schwartz, *The Complex PTSD Workbook: A Mind-Body Approach to Regaining Emotional Control and Becoming Whole* (Althea Press, 2016).

14. Heller and Kammer, *The Practical Guide*.

15. Heller and Kammer, The Practical Guide.

16. Heller and Kammer, The Practical Guide.

17. Stanley Keleman, *Emotional Anatomy* (Center Press, 1985).

18. Pete Walker, *Complex PTSD: From Surviving to Thriving* (Azure Coyote, 2013).

19. Lori Gottlieb, *Maybe You Should Talk to Someone: A Therapist, Her Therapist, and Our Lives Revealed* (Houghton Mifflin Harcourt, 2019).

20. Heller and Kammer, *The Practical Guide*.

21. Bancroft, *Why Does He Do That?*

22. Brown, MA, training session.

23. Bessel van der Kolk, *The Body Keeps the Score: Brain, Mind, and Body in the Healing of Trauma* (Viking Press, 2014).

24. Daniel J. Siegel, *Mindsight: The New Science of Personal Transformation* (Bantam Books, 2010).

CHAPTER 6: GETTING OFF THE MERRY-GO-ROUND OF INSANITY

1. Elisabeth Kubler-Ross, *Death: The Final Stage of Growth* (Simon & Schuster, 1975).

2. Lisa Aronson Fontes, "8 Common Post-Separation Domestic Abuse Tactics," Domesticshelters.org, 2022.

3. N. Jacobsen and J. Gottman, *When Men Batter Women: New Insights into Ending Abusive Relationships* (Simon & Schuster, 1998).

4. Jacobsen and Gottman, *When Men Batter Women*.

CHAPTER 7: HOW TO LEAVE SAFELY

1. N. Jacobsen and J. Gottman, *When Men Batter Women: New Insights into Ending Abusive Relationships* (Simon & Schuster, 1998).

2. "Preventing Intimate Partner Violence," Centers for Disease Control and Prevention, https://www.cdc.gov/violenceprevention/intimatepartnerviolence/fastfact.html.

3. Jennifer J. Freyd, "Violations of Power, Adaptive Blindness, and Betrayal Trauma Theory," *Feminism & Psychology* 7 (1997): 22–32.

4. Sarah J. Harsey, Eileen L. Zurbriggen, and Jennifer J. Freyd, "Perpetrator Responses to Victim Confrontation: DARVO and Victim Self-Blame," *Journal of Aggression, Maltreatment, & Trauma*, 26:6, 644-663 (2017), https://doi.org/10.1080/10926771.2017.1320777.

5. S. R. Lowe et al., "Do Levels of Posttraumatic Growth Vary by Type of Traumatic Event Experienced?," *Psychological Trauma: Theory, Research, Practice, and Policy* 14(7) (2022): 1221–1229, https://doi.org/10.1037/tra0000554.

CHAPTER 8: POST-TRAUMATIC GROWTH

1. Lundy Bancroft, *Why Does He Do That? Inside the Minds of Angry and Controlling Men* (Penguin Random House, 2002).

2. Richard G. Tedeschi and Lawrence Calhoun, "The Posttraumatic Growth Inventory: Measuring the Positive Legacy of Trauma," *Journal of Trauma Stress* 9 (1996), https://doi.org/10.1007/BF02103658.

3. Richard G. Tedeschi and Lawrence G. Calhoun, "Posttraumatic Growth: Conceptual Foundations and Empirical Evidence," *Psychological Inquiry* 15:1 (2004): 1–18, https://doi.org/10.1207/s15327965pli1501_01.

4. Laurence Heller and Brad J. Kammer, *The Practical Guide for Healing Developmental Trauma Using the Neuroaffective Relational Model to Address Adverse Childhood Experiences and Resolve Complex Trauma* (North Atlantic Books, 2022).

5. Arielle Schwartz, *The Complex PTSD Workbook: A Mind-Body Approach to Regaining Emotional Control and Becoming Whole* (Althea Press, 2016).

6. Scott Barry Kaufman and Emanuel Jauk, "Healthy Selfishness and Pathological Altruism: Measuring Two Paradoxical Forms of Selfishness," *Front Psychol* (2020), https://doi.org/10.3389/fpsyg.2020.01006.

7. Schwartz, *The Complex PTSD Workbook.*

8. Sandra L. Brown, MA, Institute for Relational Harm Online Training, 2023, http://survivortreatment.com/.

9. Brown, MA, training session.

10. Daniel J. Siegel, *Mindsight: The New Science of Personal Transformation* (Bantam Books, 2010).

11. Schwartz, *The Complex PTSD Workbook*.

12. Brown, MA, training session.

13. Julie Tseng and Jordan Poppenk, "Brain meta-state transitions demarcate thoughts across task contexts exposing the mental noise of trait neuroticism," *Nat Commun* 11, 3480 (2020), https://doi.org/10.1038/s41467-020-17255-9.

14. Pete Walker, *Complex PTSD: From Surviving to Thriving* (Azure Coyote, 2013).

15. Brown, MA, training session.

16. Brown, MA, training session.

17. Brown, MA, training session.

18. Brown, MA, training session.

19. Brown, MA, training session.

20. Walker, *Complex PTSD*.

21. Kristen Neff, *Fierce Self-Compassion: How Women Can Harness Kindness to Speak Up, Claim Their Power, and Thrive* (Harper Wave, 2021).

22. Edward R. Watkins, *Rumination Focused Cognitive Behavioral Therapy for Depression* (Guilford Press, 2018).

23. Angela Duckworth, *Grit: The Power of Passion and Perseverance* (Simon & Schuster, 2017).

CHAPTER 9: AVOIDING THE FUTURE PL

1. Terrence Real, *How Can I Get Through to You? Closing the Intimacy Gap Between Men and Women* (Scribner, 2010).

2. Terence Real, *US: Getting Past You & Me to Build a More Loving Relationship* (Rodale Books, 2002).

3. Real, *US*.

CHAPTER 10: GO LIVE

1. Jennifer Welwood, "Unconditional," https://jenniferwelwood.com/poetry/unconditional.

About the Author

....

A WOMAN WHOSE STORY RESEMBLES YOURS.

As a twenty-two-year-old, Nadine Caridi never understood what she was committing to when she married Jordan Belfort, the stockbroker infamously known as the "Wolf of Wall Street." Their eight-year marriage began as a fairy tale, filled with romantic dinners, expensive gifts, and lavish parties. But once they were bonded, Jordan's "mask" began to slip, and acts of infidelity, narcissistic abuse, insatiable greed, and uncontrollable drug addiction became Nadine's nightmare. Nadine naively believed that their connection was real and that her love could save him, so she remained trauma bonded until the pain of their relationship became too much to bear. It would be decades before she realized her story resembled thousands of other women's relational experiences.

Everything changed once she left him.

At thirty, Nadine packed up her kids and left Jordan, relocating to Los Angeles, California. She began a transformative process of intensive therapy and deep self-reflection, which required facing her pain, owning her mistakes, and reconnecting with the authentic self she'd lost due to her first marriage. A passion for helping others was born through her healing. She returned to school at thirty-nine to become a

psychotherapist and, seven years later, graduated with a PhD in counseling and somatic psychology.

Then, she found her passion and purpose.

Dr. Nae's private practice quickly flooded with women recounting
an all-too-familiar story of abuse with a pathological partner. Her goal
of helping people develop healthy relationships took on a life of its
own as she realized that trauma bonds were increasingly prevalent and
destroying the lives of hundreds of women. Nadine embarked on a
twelve-year journey of learning about domestic violence, combining
her academic background with her own experience and her patients'
experiences. This eventually led her to become an industry expert in
narcissistic abuse, trauma bonds, and complex PTSD.

Dr. Nae is a mother of five (and two dogs), a loving wife of twenty-
four years, a writer, therapist, cancer survivor, and champion of abused
women.